Aging in America

A Cautionary Tale of Wrongful Death in Elder Care

Karol Charles, JD, LLM

Aging in America: A Cautionary Tale of Wrongful Death in Elder Care

Published by Senior Care Publishing LLC USA

ISBN: 978-0-692-11689-0 (paperback)
ISBN: 978-0-692-12730-8 (ebook)
LCCN: 2018905249

rev201901

This booklet is a narrative by a daughter about the wrongful death of her mother, Rose. It is intended to help you prepare and protect yourself and those you love as you grow older. It is not a substitute for personalized advice from a professional advisor. No guarantee can be made as to the accuracy of the information contained within. Purchasing the booklet does not create any client relationship or other advisory, fiduciary, or professional services relationship with the publisher or with the author.

In order to maintain their anonymity of persons and places, in some instances, names of individuals and places may have changed. The author and publisher have made every effort to ensure that the information in this book was correct at the time of publication. The author and publisher do not assume and hereby disclaim any liability to any party for any loss, damage, or disruption caused by errors or omissions, whether such errors or omissions result from negligence, accident, or any other cause.

To Rose, my mom, who is missed every day

Contents

Appendices

Introduction

I never meant for my mom, Rose, to become a poster child for wrongful death. She always asked me if I would forget her. I always told her NO! How could I when I loved her so much? When someone you love dies—especially from a wrongful death—you never forget.

I NEVER GOT TO TELL THE TRUTH ABOUT HOW MY MOM DIED

A COVER UP OCCURRED

A JURY WOULD HAVE FOUND GUILT

On our last good day together, I put a shawl around Mom's shoulders. It was on a beautiful summer day, August 15, 2012. The activity room where she lived was cool, and I didn't want her to catch a cold. I valued her well-being every day.

That day, we had been outside in the garden for

hours talking and taking in the sun. I left her at a party happily listening to music, eating cake, and having fun.

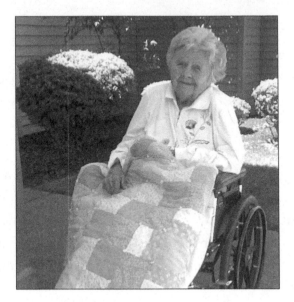

The next morning, August 16, they hurt her. It was another warm, lovely August day we should have been able to enjoy together. If they had only told the truth and done the right thing. They could have called me. Instead, they hurt her.

After that, Mom never had another nice day. I wish I could change what would happen to her that morning. The shawl I put around her shoulders could not protect her from their abuse. That's the day the Cover Up began.

This sad story about Rose, written by me, her daughter and a tax and estate planning lawyer, is told as it happened. I wrote it as a warning to learn the truth about existence for many old people in the United States. No sugar coating about how life can end. I've observed how the value of human life has changed. Do you know what a life is worth today? The truth behind this story will shock you.

Think of it this way: You will still be the same person tomorrow as you are today. You don't change inside. Growing older doesn't mean you are no longer *you*. Yes, you still have emotions and your heart can ache with hope and disappointment.

And yet, as people get old, they are not treated the same as young people. We live in a culture that doesn't respect elders. Old people are told, "You have lived a good life," and then they are pushed aside. They hurt and die, and their journey doesn't matter anymore.

Right now, tune into the way you feel and the plans you're making for the future. Suppose all of a sudden you find yourself "old." Are you ready to die? No. You still think about having fun, eating good food, taking a vacation. Then the day comes when these things won't ever happen again. You don't know when that will be, but what if it were tomorrow, next week, or next month? Are you ready for a time when no one respects you any longer? A time when you become faceless and no longer important?

That is what happened to Rose, my mom—a faceless older person who was no longer important to those entrusted to help her. It didn't matter that she was a good person. Being sweet, kind, and honest her

whole life didn't help her in the end. Rose did everything she could to deserve a pleasant old age. But she
was denied that; she deserved better.

I wanted to tell members of a jury about Mom,
and I knew they would fall for her. They would see the
warmth in her eyes and her joy of life in the videos and
photos I had ready to show them. I wanted them to
hear the cute way she'd say "Hi!" They would understand and feel she still had value; she was not worth-
less. She was smart and loved life and medicine. A
Red Cross nurse volunteer, she seemed to know more
about nursing than the nurses in the so-called "skilled"
nursing facility where she lived.

Jury members would listen and realize Rose was
a human being deserving to live. They would like her
when they learned her story.

But it never came to be. The Cover Up made sure
Rose's case didn't get that far.

PART ONE

A True Story of Neglect

1

The Tragic Story Begins

An only child, Rose never felt much love from her parents. So when she became a mother, she was determined to be a really good mom. And she was.

Mom had me in her late 30s. I also have an older brother Kelly, whom she always loved immensely. Neither of us had a father. Her two marriages ended in divorce after alcohol and gambling by both men split them apart.

Because Mom was a beauty, she had her pick in men. A great dancer in the big band era, she was full of life, yet she picked the wrong men. So, for years, it was just the three of us: Rose, my brother Kelly, and me.

Mom struggled to make ends meet as a single parent. No new clothes or dinners out, no new cars or country club outings for her.

Seniors awaiting their nutritious lunch.

Rose waits for her low-income senior lunch.

FIRED!

While still raising us, Mom got fired by the very doctors she worked for like a slave. She was a physician's assistant standing all day seeing patients and giving shots six days a week. Those long hours had rendered her joints in a degenerative condition. The doctors didn't care and weren't grateful for all she had given them over 20 years. They asked her to stay late after work one night, then with no warning, they fired her because she was getting older and slower. Rose had never been late a day to work or missed work, even in bad, snowy weather when she had to make a long drive alone in her old car.

The doctors, her employers, showed no gratitude at all. Their idea for her was to apply for social security early. Nice guys, huh, after all the money they'd made. They had no idea how much Mom struggled to make ends meet on her pitiful salary and the few benefits they provided. It seems they took advantage of a nice person and *didn't care.*

The day she was fired, by chance, I had come by in my car to meet her as a surprise. I'll never forget the stunned, traumatic, and hurt look on her face as she walked out the back door of their medical clinic, FIRED! She'd never been fired before. Why did those doctors have to hurt her feelings this way?

I guess it should have been a wakeup call to what some doctors can be like. What could she do now? Social security seemed to be her only option with no retirement plan provided by the wealthy doctors. They saved only for themselves.

Poor Mom was consumed with worry about her future at 61, knowing it was rough to start over at that age. What a blow after being a faithful employee for two decades. Instead of being rewarded, she was betrayed without even a warning. Should she have sued them? We never discussed that option. Instead, we went to Denny's for dinner—our big treat.

Who Counts in This World?

My mom's story is one of many possible tragedies facing elderly people in the United States. You work hard your whole life and do your best to save, only to have a health or economic hardship wipe you out. Social security doesn't provide much of a financial life boat. And the future of growing old and having only social security scares many. Where and how do you survive, and who will care about you?

As the old saying goes, money talks. And if you don't have it, you don't count much in this world.

Not an Encouraging Future

Unless we're wealthy, we "baby boomers" are concerned about the prospects of growing old and alone in the United States. The future doesn't look encouraging. The information is the same in all the senior, retirement, or elder care books, magazines, or seminars. We see the same celebrity pictures. We see someone trying to sell us something. Who really wants to buy life insurance? How will that help you in your old age? You can't count on long-term care insurance benefits being available from many insurers. And no one wants to tell it like it really is.

Rose's Story Tells It Like It Is

Everyone in my family trusted the people in the system to take care of Rose. They promised and acted so caring, it seemed. But the hospital staff, the doctors, the nurses, or those running the "skilled" nursing facility didn't seem to care at all in the end. Not one person in the entire medical system cared. Instead, I believe they abused, neglected, and hurt my mom.

This true story describing the end of Rose's life is about the Cover Up. Rose didn't do anything wrong. She deserved better.

What happened to Rose is documented in the medical records—records they tried to hide. It took me months to uncover them all. They also tried to delay and resist having these records discovered. It took the help of several kind lawyers for me to retrieve them all. These lawyers were a rarity in that they offered their help without asking for economic gain. They taught me the early steps to take in protecting loved ones in the event of an elder abuse or wrongful death case.

The ugly truth of what had been done to my poor mom was all documented in those records. That's why I wrote this true story about her. I hope it will help to protect you and those you love.

2

Help Me! Medical Care Denied

If it weren't for a legal settlement after mediation, we should have been in a trial January 2018. I would have told a true story to the jury. The truth was documented in the medical records and notes from the "skilled" nursing home, the hospital, and the medical director's clinic. The contents of the records were damning for them.

My brother and I were not happy with the mediation. We wanted to go to trial. Don't think when you start down the litigation path that any step of the way gets easier or better. In mediation we were negotiating with an insurance company that used every tactic to fight us.

A Survivable Stroke

Mom had a survivable stroke a minute or so before seven in the morning when the RN at the "skilled" nursing home came in to her room to check on her and have her take her morning medicine. When the aides had gotten her dressed for breakfast at six-forty-five, she was fine—but she wasn't fine a few minutes later.

The RN didn't call 911 even though there was a phone right beside Mom's bed. The records show Rose was desperately trying to catch the eyes of the aides, hoping someone would help her. But no one did. Can you imagine that?

It made me cry when I read their notes months after Rose was gone. If the RN had called 911, she would have gone to the hospital Emergency Room that was only two minutes away. If the RN had called 911, in my opinion and the opinions of many others, Rose would likely have survived. At least she would have been given the chance to survive because survival rates increase the faster a stroke is treated.

And Then They Lied

Thus began the Cover Up—abuse, abandonment, neglect, denial of care, medical negligence, and the system's efforts to mask it. They simply let her death happen. The medical caregivers and their lawyers allowed the Cover Up to be created and spun their story accordingly. Those who foster this behavior through their lawyers and the failed legal system should be ashamed and suffer miserable deaths as they caused my poor mom. That would be justice.

What happened to Rose on August 16, 2012, and how she suffered at the hands of her caregivers for 19 days was written in their records—the very records I struggled to obtain for months. Remember, on August 15, she was fine, so keep that date in mind.

The lawyer for the "skilled" nursing home took my

deposition in December of 2016. She delayed, stalled, and postponed the timeline for the case going to trial numerous times. She told us more than once that her client's representative was thinking about the amount of damages to offer us. We just needed to wait.

But this was all a lie.

The demeanor of opposing counsels at a deposition is usually not very nice. If they are nice, they're trying to trick the witness into loosening up and saying too much—into telling a story so they can twist it and use it against you later.

My Deposition

The goal of the "skilled" nursing home's lawyer was to find out how damaging I would be as a witness at the trial of my mom's case. The lawyer didn't like what I had to say under oath. But I told the truth, unlike those who represented the nursing home.

An excerpt below from my deposition's testimony—taken by the lawyer for the "skilled" nursing home's insurance company—reveals some of what they learned through my testimony. I didn't say anything to help them; I just told the awful truth.

The deposition was in December of 2016, more than four years after we lost Rose. I thought we still had a chance for the truth to come out before the trial. The lawyer for "skilled" nursing used my deposition as a basis to arm its hired expert with new lies as they got ready for the mediation in two months.

This excerpt will give you the flavor of a deposition. The lawyer (highly paid by the insurance company for "skilled" nursing) asked the questions that follow. The answers are mine.

Q. Did you keep a journal or any kind of notes contemporaneous with the events in August of 2012?[1]
A. No. I remember everything in my head.

Q. So you can remember all of these details in your head?
A. Something of such major importance as this, yes. I found out from the medical records in 2013 that the morning of my mom's stroke (or apparent stroke), the aides went in, got her dressed for breakfast in one of her favorite birthday shirts—she was able to pick out which shirt she wanted to put on—a bracelet, which I happen to have on today, that was one of hers. And when the RN, Cheryl, came in and discovered her in the process of the stroke—I'm saying—my mom was looking at the aides trying to get eye contact with them, trying to speak, desperate to get some help, and she was ignored. It was pretty callous. Pretty unforgiving, again, for a seven-year resident when you're trusting these people.

---

1 The lawyer for "skilled" nursing asked if I kept a journal or any kind of written notes. If you keep contemporaneous notes or a journal, this can help you later. It helps you prove what really happened as opposed to "skilled" nursing being able to later change or create its own records. See my comments in Access to Medical Records in Part Two.

Q. And were you present?

A. No. I read this in the medical record.

Q. And that version of events you read in "skilled nursing's" medical records?

A. Yes.

Q. Do you have any other examples that you can recall to support the contention that your mom was not given consideration, respect, or full recognition of her dignity?

A. From reading from the medical records and finding out that my mom did not have swallowing capacity, I read where an RN was saying she would get food down my mom by putting it in the back of her mouth, triggering a gag reaction, so basically they were putting food so far back that it would go down, even if she was gagging. I didn't know that until I got the medical records, and I think that's pretty awful.

Q. Did you ever follow up with anyone who conducted that investigation for the State on that issue, the feeding issue?

A. I spoke with the DSHS people several times. They called me after their investigation. I don't recall that particular one. I know the one woman said to me, "It's very hard for us to find something or catch them if the resident is already dead, isn't it." That was her comment.

Q. Any other examples that come to you memory regarding factual support for the contention that your mom was not given consideration, respect, and full recognition of her dignity?

A. On Saturday, August 18, I arrived at "skilled" nursing in the morning and was told by the nurse, an RN, and the Vietnamese male aide who had been a history teacher in Vietnam, that my mom had eaten breakfast, that he had fed her breakfast and juice, and they were ecstatic; they were happy. They were making me feel good. And then at lunch, another RN came down to the room to feed her lunch with the aides, and I left the room while they were doing that so my mom would eat her food.

In the records—faxes from the lab on my mom acquired through the hospital records—I found out that, before lunch, the RN at the "skilled" nursing had received a fax from the lab that there was no UTI. The report said there was no growth. [That meant] the "skilled" nursing and the medical director and his clinic had misdiagnosed her. She never had a UTI. The fax from the lab went to them, and none of them did anything. After lunch, the RN faxed the nurse practitioner at the medical director's clinic saying this: "There might be a possible stroke." Meanwhile, they're feeding my mom, continuing to give her antibiotics, and they're documenting there is no UTI and there might be a stroke. I think it's pretty awful what they did to my mom, and I was there at the time, and they never alerted me or my brother about the fax from the lab.

Q. Any other examples that you have a memory of that support your contention that your mom was not given consideration, respect, and full recognition of her dignity?
A. I'm thinking what days I've not covered. I think I've done the 16th. I could go through each day. It's hard to remember which ones I haven't done. On August 17th, she was given an antibiotic injection into the muscle, as opposed to the oral one they had given her the night before, and it's Rocephin. They didn't explain that antibiotic to us.

The night before, they had said it was very strong. They didn't explain its side effects, possible damage, things to be concerned about. They just gave it to her. And I later found out through research that this drug can aggravate, if not cause, a stroke by some medical studies. It's probably one of the most extremely painful injections, even more than tetanus, that a person can receive, and the effects of it can last for weeks. I think that was a pretty awful thing to do to a woman who was in distress and suffering and not even to explain that potential damage and pain it would cause.

Q. To whom?
A. My mother.

Q. Explain it to her?
A. The pain of an injection that could last 18 days or weeks.

Q. How do you know they didn't?
A. I was there.

Q. The whole time?
A. When they gave the injection.

Q. Any other factual examples to support the contention that your mom was not given consideration, respect, and full recognition of her dignity?
A. She had a very old POLST (Physician's Order for Life-Sustaining Treatment), never been updated to reflect desires that we—we, my brother and I and she—had made. Even with the old POLST they were using, it requested IV fluids, and if they could not be administered, transport to the hospital. They barely got an IV in on Friday, August 17th, to try and keep her hydrated a bit, because she was very sleepy, and it was a heat wave. The IV came out later that night. They didn't call us. They didn't let us know. They didn't transport her to the hospital. I remember reading in the records, I think the nurse practitioner had ordered a 24-hour drip, but the request for health care that was at least in the file, even though it was an old POLST, requested an IV for fluids, and if they were not able to do it, to transport to the hospital. So the short term, it was in, and it came out. They didn't call us; they didn't

transport her to the hospital. They continued to try and force fluid down her throat. And then by Sunday, the 19th, they totally abandoned her without anything. So that's another example of pretty awful treatment. I'm not using the exact same words that are in that clause. You've asked me so many examples, it's hard to remember the original question.

Q. That's fine. With respect to the POLST you've identified, what are you referring to as being an old POLST, never updated?
A. The POLST that was in her file was done in 2009 by the Evercare person who actually caused all the harm to my mom in 2010. We had that person taken off the file. I think Evercare may have fired the person. "Skilled" nursing didn't even think to update POLSTs after what that person had done. My mom went out of "skilled" nursing 2010 to the hospital where we had a feeding tube for safety for her. Then when she came back to "skilled" nursing, her POLST should have been updated every time she went in or out to reflect current desires. It would have reflected the feeding tube, intravenous, antibiotics. None of that was updated in the POLST.

Q. Any other examples that fit the category of factual information that supports a contention that your mother was not given consideration, respect, or full recognition of her dignity?
A. Another example would be Sunday, August 19th

when my brother and I received no call from "skilled" nursing. We arrived there Sunday morning and found my mom totally abandoned, in her bed, by the nursing staff, all food, all liquid, everything taken away from her, a sign on the wall like something to the effect, "Nothing to be administered." Totally left and abandoned alone in her room. They had made no call to us. My mom was scared. She was in her bed. Nobody was helping her. So my brother and I arrived, and if we hadn't gone over there, I don't know how long that would have gone on.

Q. Did you speak with anyone about that?
A. Yes.

Q. Who did you speak with?
A. My brother was yelling at the RN, who was supposed to be taking care of my mom. My brother and I both ran down the hall asking for help to another RN.

Q. Anything else? Anyone else?
A. Those were the two RNs we were dealing with, asking for help, and we were insisting my mom be sent to the hospital. She had been clearly abandoned.

Q. On what date?
A. Sunday, August 19th.

Two months after my deposition, we had to go to mediation by court requirements before a trial.

The mediation date was set for February of 2017 because the trial was supposed to be in April of 2017. (Remember, Rose lost her life in September of 2012.)

The actual record of what happened at the "skilled" nursing facility was presented by our lawyer in our mediation[2] brief as follows in italics:

On Wednesday, August 15, 2012, Rose was a resident at "skilled" nursing. Rose ate dinner that night and communicated normally. The next morning, August 16, 2012, the RN for "skilled" nursing, found Rose in her bed uncommunicative with her eyes affixed and her arm in the air—she appeared to be paralyzed.

"Skilled" nursing staff, including registered nurses, failed to notice the obvious signs and symptoms of a stroke. Instead, over the next four days they led Rose's family to believe that she was in a non-emergent condition, that she only had a urinary tract infection, and that they had the ability to care for her. Also over those next four days the staff continued to try to feed Rose and force pills down her throat, even though Rose clearly could not swallow. (See Appendix A for an

2   Mediation is required before you go to trial. It gave the lawyers for "skilled" nursing a chance to arm their expert witness with more lies. The mediation session took place two months after their lawyers took my deposition. An excerpt from my deposition follows these mediation excerpts, shown in italic.

email from a retired doctor friend told the story how Mom suffered at the hands of "skilled" nursing. This happened almost a year after Rose's death. It was sent to me on Monday, August 12, 2013, at 2:18 p.m.) Rose was in a paralyzed state and although conscious she was unable to tell the "skilled" nursing staff what they were doing was killing her. Their actions led to Rose suffering a significant deterioration of her overall condition.

Finally on Sunday, August 19, 2012, when it became apparent to Rose's family that "skilled" nursing was not providing proper care to Rose, her family took matters into their own hands and requested that she be hospitalized. The pain and stress of this neglect caused a speedy decline in Rose's overall health, including the development of aspiration pneumonia, ultimately resulting in her death on September 4, 2012.

Rose was denied prompt and adequate care, was not promptly transferred to the hospital, suffered unnecessary pain and ultimately had her life shortened by the negligence of the staff of "skilled" nursing.

There is no denying Rose suffered a left hemispheric stroke on the morning of August 16, 2012 based on the radiologic/CT examinations of her head on August 20, 2012 at the hospital. The area of damage directly correlated with the right side paralysis and dysphagia that Rose was diagnosed with upon admission to the hospital on August 19, 2012. The effects of the stroke would have been less severe and survivable had Rose been sent to the hospital the morning of August 16, 2012 by "skilled" nursing.

Furthermore, "skilled" nursing's staff negligently continued to attempt to provide Rose with hydration and nutrition orally despite documented signs of her inability to swallow, beginning the morning of August 16, 2012, which caused the aspiration pneumonia that Rose was diagnosed with upon admission to the hospital on August 19, 2012. (Aspiration pneumonia was the first cause of death listed on Rose's death certificate.)

Rose's family (her daughter Karol and son Kelly) were dedicated to her health and welfare at "skilled" nursing visiting her almost every day. Her family relied on the expertise and medical knowledge of "skilled" nursing's staff to provide them with accurate and timely updates about her condition. This was not done and ultimately Rose's life was cut short due to the negligence of "skilled" nursing.

On its website, "skilled" nursing represents itself as a "family owned" company that follows "Christian principles of caring and

compassion. True service to others. Honesty.
Integrity. Love. It's not just what we do; it's
who we are."

This is not the experience that Rose
received in her final days there.

If the deposition and mediation excerpts do not tell you what an awful place "skilled" nursing turned out to be on August 16, 17, 18, and 19 of 2012, read on to learn how we had to fight with "skilled" nursing to even have her sent to the hospital. Then you will see how the Cover Up continued with their medical director and his partners at the hospital.

Nursing Home Abuse

This a story you wouldn't think could ever happen. But it does in nursing home abuse and wrongful death situations.

The morning of August 19, 2012, we found Mom lying alone and abandoned in her bed. My brother Kelly had arrived before me, and he was desperate to find someone to help. I had stopped to buy flowers for Mom. When I arrived, I found Kelly in a panic trying to get someone's attention. The staff on duty knew she needed help and did nothing.

Specifically, the RN in charge of Rose had taped a sign on the wall beside her bed not to give Rose any food or liquid. The IV in her arm that we'd requested two days before had come out, and there was no staff member on duty who could put one in her arm again.

It was during a heat wave, and Rose would be dehydrated. She wasn't getting any of her medicine.

We asked a different RN to call for someone to put in an IV and she said the nurses were all off for the weekend. She offered no help or solution. We asked her to call an ambulance and have Rose sent to the ER. All she offered was to move Rose to the Medicare wing where one more nurse was on duty. The administrator for this "skilled" nursing facility had told this RN during a Friday afternoon meeting that Rose could be moved to the Medicare wing on the weekend but we weren't informed about that on Friday.

It was a Sunday so they were short-staffed and it seems they couldn't be bothered. Even though our local phone numbers were posted on the wall above her bed, the phone by her bedside was never used to call us. It would have been easy to just call.

Kelly and I couldn't believe how we found our mother. Yet none of the staff did anything to help her, even after we pleaded with the nurses to do so.

Imagine! The hospital was only two minutes away. Why hadn't they called an ambulance for her? Why did we have to argue with them when she clearly needed care? Because they wanted to keep her there as part of the Cover Up. We just didn't know it then.

Finally, one of the nurses, Donna, made the call to summon an ambulance, but she stalled and delayed, then called it in as a non-emergency. That was a blow to Mom's chances for fast medical care. In fact, the ambulance personnel didn't think the situation was dire and neither did the hospital staff when she arrived.

The nurses who left Rose abandoned that morning were all RNs. Until then, I thought being a registered nurse meant something.

My brother and I trusted that the RN designation reflected a high standard of caring or competency. Not so—and we learned this too late. A person can get a nursing or RN designation from even a junior college. So don't be fooled by the designation of an RN. Good nurses are few and hard to find.

Especially be wary of RNs or any nurse who works in a "skilled" nursing facility. In my experience, it's fraudulent to suggest they possess any nursing skill. Instead, we found incompetency and a lack of caring. Even as they fake being caring, they can be cold and impersonal. One or two rare treasures of a nurse may pop up in that system, but "don't count on it" is the better rule.

The RNs had left our poor mom abandoned in her bed with no medical care, food, or water, and they considered that a non-emergency. The RN named Donna kept saying the ER would not keep Rose, that the staff would just send her back. Clearly, she wanted Rose to stay in her room and not go to the ER.

The Cover Up was in full play and we still didn't know it.

Cruel and Uncaring

If this had not happened, I would not have believed these nurses would have been so cruel and uncaring. We had spent seven years getting to know, trust, and rely on them. Each of us had made a point to be personable to all of the staff—aides and nurses alike. The RN, Donna, had spent at least three of Mom's birthday celebrations with our family. How much closer and caring could a nurse be?

All of a sudden, they became cold and indifferent.

Mom had trusted Donna until the very end, and so did Kelly and I. But she also betrayed Rose. Later, we found out she was a part of the Cover Up too. That really hurt. Certainly, she was concerned about her job and her family. In the end, she didn't care about Rose at all. It makes us doubt all the paid people we've ever trusted.

Finally, Rose made the two-minute drive to the ER in an ambulance. But because Donna called it in as a non-emergency, Mom did not get priority attention in the ER. She waited there for the doctor with my brother and me almost six hours! Weak, hungry, and thirsty, she wanted to tell anyone what had happened to her. At least in the ER, we all thought there was hope.

Mom felt relieved to be at the hospital where someone would surely help her. When the doctor finally arrived, she smiled at him with her cute smile. The multitude of medical records for Rose all document the case of a pleasant, frail woman with the cutest smile. To this day, people remember that smile.

But despite her smile and bright, attentive eyes that trusted and relied on them, she turned out to be the person no one helped. I can still see her eyes—full of life—trustingly reaching out to the medical personnel who came into her room.

I wanted the jury to know that Rose dearly wanted to live.

But the doctor was not smiling. He looked at us and asked why she had not come sooner. Who had kept her for so many days when she needed help? We explained to the doctor that on August 16, the RNs at "skilled" nursing told us that: 1) Rose had an infection, 2) they had called the doctor who was the medical director for the facility, 3) he had ordered a lab and antibiotics for her, and 4) the people on staff emphasized they could take care her. Then three days later on August 19, we found her totally abandoned in her bed. Rose had been asking for help. But no one at the facility showed an interest in her situation.

The ER doctor shook his head and sighed. "Oh, yes," he said. "This is what they're doing now if you are poor. The nursing facilities won't always help someone; they ignore their cries for help. They don't call for an ambulance when it's needed."

We were stunned. "Why?" we asked the doctor, fearing he would send her back to the facility. Where could she go to get good care?

"It's the money," the doctor explained. "Corporate greed has taken over and is causing harm and abuse with aging and vulnerable adults. The corporate-owned facilities make the money when they don't call the ambulance. (See Appendix B for a report from Douglas Perednia, MD, that explains the situation.) They don't want the hospital to make that money for treatment because the nursing facility gets paid if the hospital doesn't get paid. It's the new trend in the economics of aging, and it's not very nice. This is happening all over the country."

Too Late to Be Saved

The doctor's expression was cold when he said in front of Rose it was too late for her to be saved. He wasn't even trying. I thought it was shocking he would say that when Rose was trying to smile at him and show him she wanted to live.

Imagine! We were in a hospital ER and still the doctor didn't care. He seemed bothered to have to come to the ER, called away from an outdoor barbeque, his breath smelling of beer. He didn't care that Rose was hungry and dehydrated. He didn't care that her blood pressure was 200[3] and her head was pounding.

---

3   The top number refers to the amount of pressure in your arteries during contraction of your heart muscle. This is called systolic pressure. The bottom number refers to your blood pressure when your heart muscle is between beats. This is called diastolic pressure. Normal blood pressure is under 120/80. From 120/80 to 139/89 is pre-hypertension. The threshold for high blood pressure is 140/90, while anything over 180/110 is hypertensive crisis–an emergency.

Looking back, I still hate him knowing he purposely didn't help her.

The "skilled" nursing's medical director's office was across the street from the hospital and only a five-minute walk from the facility. The doctor who came to the ER was a partner of the medical director (a stranger to us) who had stopped by their office on his way to the ER. There, he found a fax from the lab about Rose. Dated August 18, 2012, it had been sent to the "skilled" nursing home and also to his office. However, no one in his office had responded to the fax. He didn't even tell us about the fax. Maybe that's why he was cruel to our mom.

He, too, was part of the Cover Up.

Finally Admitted to the Hospital

Finally, after being rude and hurtful, this doctor agreed to admit Mom to the hospital that night. This was almost *10 hours* since we had found Rose abandoned in her bed. And for 10 hours, we'd been trying to get someone to help her. Can you believe you can be treated this way if you have a medical emergency? Is this really the United States?

Rose woke up in the tiniest shared room on a general administration floor of the hospital. The nurses called me around seven o'clock to let me know she'd asked for coffee. I thought that meant she was better. Then they put her on the phone to say "Hi" in that cute little voice. (I had recorded that so the jury could hear her voice say "Hi!")

There was no special care on this floor, but it's where the doctor had placed her the night before. Again, he seemingly didn't care about helping her. We didn't realize she was put on the wrong floor on purpose until it was too late.

Rose had been in this hospital before on floors that provided more care. Some floors provided special care for specific medical conditions and nurses who really made the effort to help. Why was Rose admitted by the doctor to a small, shared room with no special care this time? We were confused.

The nurse explained that this was not like private hospitals for the advantaged: politicians, celebrities, and athletes. Well, what she said may have been true, but it was still confusing. Rose had been on better floors before at this hospital.

Later, we discovered this was part of the Cover Up—that is, put Rose on a floor where she will not get the care she needs—the care she should have received days earlier if she had not been abused and neglected by those she trusted to help her.

We believe that if the doctor had put her on a floor for the type of care she needed, she would have survived. Yet we didn't know she'd never have a chance on this floor. We kept clinging to the hope she'd get better. Surely, she'd be okay in the hospital. But she wasn't.

Can you imagine this happening to you or someone you love?

On August 20, that first morning in the hospital, Rose had asked for coffee. She was happy and felt safe. All she wanted was to drink coffee and feel good again. Rose loved her coffee.

But the hospital nurses said "no coffee." What? All Rose wanted was coffee; what a simple request! After all, it had been five days since her last cup of coffee because she never made it to breakfast on August 16 to eat and enjoy that cup of coffee.

Sadly, she never got to have that cup of coffee in the hospital—or ever again.

Think of the cup of coffee you drank this morning. What if it were your last one? Every morning when I make my coffee, I look at the clock and think of Rose asking for coffee that first morning in the hospital. It is a reminder I'll never get over—how a simple pleasure in life can be taken away just like that. Worst of all, it was taken from her by people she trusted. Who could do that to you one day?

On August 28, the doctor discharged Rose from the hospital and sent her back to the "skilled" nursing facility. He didn't tell us all the results of her tests in the hospital. But we did find out she didn't have the infection that the "skilled" nursing personnel told us she had. It was confirmed she had suffered a small, survivable ischemic stroke at seven in the morning on August 16.

After the aides had dressed her and when the RN

came in to assist her would have been the time to call 911 that morning to restore her health. Instead, a misdiagnose and sloppy care that gave her sepsis caused her suffering and a slow death. The ER doctor never told us she'd been admitted to the hospital with sepsis.

This medical partner doctor was also a part of the Cover Up for the medical director and their office. Sadly, after Rose was discharged from the hospital, not one doctor from that practice came to see her— not even the medical director for the "skilled" nursing facility. He didn't care.

But he did sign her death certificate, the heartless bastard, without ever having seen her.

"She's Gone"

That morning when my house phone rang at five-forty-five in the morning won't ever be forgotten.[4] It was the call I dreaded. A cold, impersonal voice over the phone said the worst news anyone could bear to hear: "She's gone." The pain never goes away from that cold detached voice that came so early in the day.

Later that day, we went over to "skilled" nursing to get mom's personal belongings and her birthday balloons. There beside her bed was her empty wheelchair. A tragic reminder of what had happened earlier that day. There was nothing more painful than the sight

---

4 The "skilled" nursing personnel never called me except for the morning we lost Rose. We had a private phone right beside her on her table for calls to either my brother or me. Yet, the morning of August 16, they didn't call us. We would have had Rose sent to the ER, and I believe she would have lived.

of an empty wheelchair where once had been our mom so full of life. Rose had left this world that morning with all her birthday balloons still inflated around her. Birthday balloons for a dear person celebrating life.

3

It Goes by so Fast

Nineteen years and 19 days. The number 19 in numerology stands for the beginning and the end. Rose's retirement was 19 years and her end-of-life struggle was 19 days.

There's now a huge emptiness without her. I miss her smile, her warm voice, her very being. My best friend is gone. They took her from us. It wasn't a natural death; it was a wrongful death.

What Really Happened to Rose?

Rose was fine until the morning of August 16th, they day they hurt her. Tragically, the records show she woke up feeling good and the aides dressed her for breakfast in a favorite birthday shirt—one she'd only worn once after her birthday. It had never even been washed. I kept that shirt hoping to show it to the jury, along with a photo of her with all her inflated birthday balloons.

Full of life, Rose was looking forward to our continuing celebration of her birthday, which had been

July 26. In early August, we went out to lunch and planned more outings. I had made a poster with all the pictures from her birthday party. When I brought it to her room and hung it on the wall, the aides raced in to see it. They told her how good she looked, saying she'll have many more birthdays. She smiled. "I hope so," she said. I also wanted the jury to see that poster.

As I was hanging it, the activity volunteer came in to tell me about a surprise she and several residents had planned for Rose that August. They had voted her as the First Resident, which meant she'd have a large photo framed and hung in the lobby of the facility. Mom would have been surprised and pleased to see how other residents cared about her.

But she never got to enjoy that surprise.

It is unfair that her chance for a moment of happiness was taken from her. They should have been exposed and paid a price for what they did to her.

A week after the poster was hung, the aides had dressed Rose for breakfast. That was on the 16th, the day the nursing staff hurt her. The records show Rose desperately tried to catch the eye of an aide to help her, but the person looked the other way because, according to facility rules, aides weren't allowed to assist.

That makes no sense. At the least, someone should have called me. I wanted to tell the jury this while showing photos of the phone by Rose's bed—the phone no one used. In fact, after we lost Rose, I learned that one of the aides kept telling the RN to call me, but the RN ignored her. Yet during the investigation, this aide later lied when she said to investigators she never told the RN to call me.

Rose was never mean or cranky with any of the aides, nurses, or doctors when they came into her room. She always hoped for the best, was nice to them, and believed they'd help her. Every time an aide, nurse, or doctor came in, she smiled that cute little smile everyone commented on.

That morning, she asked them for help the best she could. Rose was frantically trying to catch the eye of any aide and trying to mouth the words "help me." When investigated, the aide denied ever telling me this information. But Rose's attempts for help were documented in the notes from "skilled" nursing that I later received. What more can a person do?

The notes from the hospital doctor and those made by the aides and nurses from the "skilled" facility commented on Rose's sweetness and kindness. She'd smile when they helped her. Even the cleaning staff told me she was nice to them, never barking orders or being cross.

In the end, none of those good traits helped Rose— the person who was abused, neglected, and hurt on August 16.

For 19 days, she fought to stay alive against the worst odds. But not even her spirit could defeat the abuse she had suffered. Her last words were "rub my head, please rub my head."

Cards Stacked Against Us

Don't be fooled. The cover ups that happen in the medical and legal system are huge. People want to protect their backs and their pocket books any way they can. That's why wrongful death law suits happen often. And the cards are stacked against the consumer.

Consider the role of the medical director in Rose's case. Nursing homes are required by state law (at least in most states) to have a medical director. They advertise credentials and convey a false confidence that they've hired doctors who care and pay attention to the residents. Ideally, every director has a big heart and cares about seniors. Yet, few ever visit their patients or meet with the families. There isn't big money in doing this!

At Rose's "skilled" nursing facility, the medical

director was semi-retired and had joined a medical clinic for the bucks—easy money for him. He never came to see Rose in the "skilled" nursing facility. He never even saw her when she experienced a serious change in her condition. But he made a wrong diagnosis, his office ordered antibiotics she didn't need, and in particular, it was an antibiotic that caused her pain from injecting it. Then he took a long weekend break and never reviewed the faxes from the lab or supervised his staff members who were supposedly on call.

What's more, he didn't walk down the street from the hospital to the "skilled" nursing facility even after Rose was released from hospital when her medical condition had declined significantly.

Imagine! In 19 days, this director didn't once see Rose. How hard is it to take a five-minute walk down the street to "skilled" nursing? It seems he had no heart or feeling for my mother as a human—even when she asked for help from his partner who had admitted her into the hospital.

That's why I call it a Cover Up. They all knew they had screwed up. Each of the medical professionals in the medical director's office failed her.

Medical director: The medical director on August 16, 2012, ordered a urinalysis for the lab STAT at 10 a.m. after the RN's call from "skilled" nursing (by the medical records, Rose's stroke started around 7 a.m.). The medical director made a diagnosis of a UTI (urinary tract infection) without seeing Rose. Even when the lab test didn't show up by noon at his office as it should have when ordered STAT at 10 a.m., he didn't call to check why it was late. The RN who called the medical director finally took the urinalysis sample for the lab at 3 p.m. Lab results came back around 5 p.m. The medical director had left early that Thursday for a long weekend off. He never came to see Rose during the 19 days she lived. And yet this medical director signed her death certificate. How could he when he never saw her? He hid behind his MD façade and acted as if he cared, then billed out his time to the "skilled" nursing facility through Medicare.

Nurse practitioner: Only the nurse practitioner for the medical director's clinic was there at 5 p.m. on August 16, 2012, to receive the fax from the lab. It showed very little sign of any infection, and yet the nurse practitioner ordered oral antibiotics for Rose. This order was made despite the records from "skilled" nursing showing that Rose had trouble swallowing and was drooling out. On Friday August 17, 2012, the nurse practitioner ordered a stronger antibiotic for Rose. This was before any lab results were back. The initial lab report had shown little if any infection.

Two doctor partners of the medical director: Neither partner of the medical director helped Rose's chances to survive or were totally honest with us.

Partner number one who came to the ER Sunday August 19, 2012, had stopped by his office on his way to the ER. He didn't tell us there was a fax from "skilled" nursing on August 18, 2012 that said likely stroke. He didn't tell us that the lab had faxed the medical clinic on August 18, 2012 showing no infection and no UTI. What he did tell us was that Rose should have come to the ER three days before. That would have been August 16, the day of her stroke. He told us she would not survive. He did not tell us why. He was so cruel in front of Rose that I complained to the ER desk. Once Rose was admitted to the hospital, I asked the nurses to have another doctor come see her. I told them how mean he had been. The nurses at the hospital told me he was from the medical director's clinic and that I should call the clinic and have them send a different doctor. I did call the clinic and ask for a different doctor.

Partner number two came Monday August 20, 2012. He too didn't tell us about the faxes that came to their clinic on Saturday. We still all thought that Rose had a UTI. This doctor ordered tests for Rose that night but no special care in her room. The next day, he told us Rose did not have a UTI but rather had suffered from a stroke sometime before. He was very vague and elusive as to when this stroke occurred. He suggested it might have been weeks before. He left Rose in her room on the general administration floor and offered no help at the hospital for someone who had suffered a stroke. He also failed to tell us that Rose had been admitted from "skilled" nursing with sepsis. The hospital had a progressive care unit where strokes and sepsis can be treated. We all were shocked to be told Rose had no UTI but instead had suffered a stroke. Mom was ready to cry over this news. But she was brave and ready to live. We talked about the diagnosis and actually watched some TV together.

No Announcement of New Director

To be fair, a good, caring medical director once worked at this "skilled" nursing facility. He had sent Rose to the ER more than once and even gave me his cell phone number. But then he took a position at a facility that wanted a physician on site, so he left.

When the good doc left, the "skilled" nursing facility didn't send out any notice to our family about the change. We didn't even receive the online newsletter "skilled" nursing later posted announcing a new medical director. Who knows how often it's published? Maybe once a year?

Instead, a note could have been sent to all patients and their families or at least posted a sign in the lobby. But no, we didn't know a new director had started.

Play It Smart from the Start

In case there's an emergency, there should be someone competent who thinks and could at least call 911 for an ambulance to take a resident to the ER. It shouldn't be that hard—but for Rose it was.

Beware of this happening to your family. You can't

let down your guard of trust regarding the nurses, staff, administrators, physicians, and all those associated with a facility. They could be as cold as ice with little concern or care in helping a senior.

If I had only realized how cold the people in this facility were *and* that they would lie, hide records, even destroy them. How could I know that, if I sued, they would hire a lawyer who summons paid experts to lie.

The cards are stacked against you unless you play it smart from the start. Prepare to protect yourself and the ones you love. If you don't do it now, it can be too late.

Why People Fight

Rarely do people sue for wrongful death for the money. They're fighting an injustice, fighting for the memory of the person they love whose life was wrongfully cut short by their actions or inactions.

My brother and I have gone through a painful experience that never can be erased. Those who have lost a loved one due to the neglect, negligence, or intentional act of others understand what a wrongful death feels like. The emotional and psychological pain makes the whole body ache. And the doubt doesn't quit. I keep thinking, "If I could only have protected her from what was coming her way."

What is Wrongful Death?

Wrongful death was explained to me by one of the lawyers who helped me in this way: "Your loved one died. You cannot function. You cannot stop crying. You cannot stop thinking about your beloved. Your world seems like it is ending. On top of this, there is awareness that someone may have caused this death. Death came too soon because someone did something either negligently or on purpose. And it is not right. You are not a greedy person. You do not want to make money off your beloved's death. But you want whomever is responsible to be held accountable. You want the world to say your loved one's death was not in vain. Your loved one was not invisible. Your loved one was worthy of being treated with dignity and respect, according to the law."

Four good lawyers helped me. It took me years to meet the right ones. Most want an easy, high-paying case. Few care about the abuse or death of an older person, especially because a person's economic value drops with age in the legal system. That's why caregivers can get away with murder—literally.

I was hurt by the way the guilty parties covered up the truth about Rose's death. Even as a lawyer myself, I was shocked and sickened to experience how the legal system worked to protect the actions of the guilty. It added salt to my wound.

When questioning Mom's untimely death, those responsible looked me in the face and lied. And then they lied under oath. They hid and destroyed documents. They paid experts to lie. The insurance lawyers worked to protect their guilty client so the insurance company wouldn't have to pay.

The value of a life is reduced by these lies. It's apparent in an elder abuse and wrongful death law suit. It's all part of the Cover Up.

Protecting Families from Elder Abuse

I write today to warn people about what they can and must do to protect themselves and those they love. They includes steps you might not think of until it's too late and documents you must have in order and kept current.

I hope you'll remember Rose and what happened to her. I learned the hard way how I might have gotten them cornered on their lies and neglect—but I learned too late.

My brother and I wanted to go to trial, but their Cover Up was in full play. If only I had known then what I know now, they would have been exposed. My consolation is to pass on to you what we've learned.

We can't change yesterday. We can hope for a better tomorrow. Dreams don't always come true.

4

Honor Rose by Taking Action

Rose always asked me if I would forget her, and I always answered NO! And neither will the people who are helped by her story.

I encourage you to have these documents completed and kept current:

- Living will
- Durable power of attorney for health care and/or financial decisions
- POLST

The living will is an advance directive, also known as a physician's directive. This documents your desires for treatment in the event of a medical emergency. The living will is typically done when you are young, healthy, and able to make your own decisions.

A durable power of attorney for health care and/or financial decisions is another type of advance directive that authorizes another person to make decisions for you if you are unable.

A POLST—Physicians Order for Life-Sustaining Treatment—is a medical directive for when you get old or have a life-threatening illness. The POLST form is a medical order indicating a person's wishes regarding treatments commonly used in a medical emergency. The POLST is the document emergency medical care providers rely on to give or withhold medical treatment. It speaks for you when you cannot speak for yourself in a medical emergency, and it should be kept current at all times. Life becomes more precious with each year and a person's wishes change. If these documents are not kept current or followed correctly by those you rely on, your wishes may evaporate at the time of an emergency.

The "skilled" nursing facility required Rose to sign a POLST, but the people entrusted to her care didn't follow her POLST guidelines. Bluntly, she didn't get the care she deserved that could have saved her life. They failed her. Worst of all, they lied and tried to sweep the truth about her death under the rug while I strive to keep the memory of Rose alive.

To get yourself and your loved ones organized, Part 2 of this book features basic, easy-to-understand information and examples of the documents listed here. They have short, clear explanations of how they can help you. Also discussed is the importance of having timely access to, and copies of, all medical records, tests, and notes from all medical caregivers, including an autopsy report.

Please know these are not provided as legal advice but rather as invaluable painful experiences of Rose.

Part Two also includes:

- summary of the Abuse of Vulnerable Adult Statute as enacted in many states today
- information on an Elder Abuse and Wrongful Death case
- actual example of a Wrongful Death Complaint

The names of some have been changed or removed to protect the guilty.

PART TWO

Forms and Information

As I write this, it is five-and-a-half years after we lost Rose. We were supposed to go to trial in January of 2018. That's how long the lawyers for the "skilled" nursing facility stretched it out. Using every trick to delay, they figured that, if enough time went by, we would forget details and not be as emotionally raw when testifying.

They would have been wrong. We wanted to go to trial. We have not forgotten anything. That's why I can write this story today.

How could something as awful and obvious in the records of what they did to her get swept away? It was so painful to read them and see the probable cause of her death. I go over and over the situation in my mind. I can hear her words "Help Me" over and over.

Our lawyer knew abuse occurred, too, which is why he took on the case. A good man and a good lawyer, he believes in the rights of older people to live. Rose should have lived.

Those running the facility did get by with it to a

certain extent. They paid their insurance company lawyer to get them off with a settlement they could afford and which kept their reputation intact in the community. They would have faced negative exposure at a trial.

Clearly, this was not a caring, competent Christian environment with highly skilled RNs as advertised. Their lawyer paid an expert witness enough to make it impossible to prove that those involved were wrong. In fact, new lies popped up every time we advanced a position against them. It all tied into the death certificate the medical director for the "skilled" nursing had signed.

Because we had trusted them, we didn't grab the evidence at the moment when we should have. Trusting them cost Rose her life. She pleaded for help, but they betrayed her. I hear her voice to this day.

Critical Documents

In Part Two, I explain critical documents you must have as you age and the importance of keeping them current. If you have a loved one gone from a suspected wrongful death, read the synopsis and snapshot from a personal account of what it's like to be in a wrongful death lawsuit. Dreams don't always come true.

Perhaps one of the most important lessons to learn from Rose's story is knowing you have the right to immediate access to medical records. You must review them daily, get copies, and make sure the record is preserved before others destroy, hide, or change them.

You'll also find documents and information with my personal thoughts in Part Two. They're not given as legal advice but shared from the heart to help you.

1

Living Will Example

Definition: A health care directive, living will, is a legal document which specifies a person's desires regarding the care they receive at the end of their life if that person is unable to communicate those desires. This document is completed when a person is younger and still in good health. In one state, the living will is only used if the person has a terminal condition and life-sustaining treatment will only artificially prolong the process of dying; or, if the person is in an irreversible coma and there is no reasonable hope of recovery.

Directive made this _____ day of
_____, 20___.

I, _____, being of sound mind, willfully, and voluntarily make known my desire that my dying shall not be artificially prolonged under the circumstances set forth below, and do hereby declare that:

1) If at any time I should have an incurable and irreversible condition certified to be a terminal

condition by my attending physician, and where the application of life-sustaining treatment would serve only to artificially prolong the process of my dying, I direct that such treatment be withheld or withdrawn, and that I be permitted to die naturally. I understand "terminal condition" means an incurable and irreversible condition caused by injury, disease or illness that would, within reasonable medical judgment, cause death within a reasonable period of time in accordance with accepted medical standards.

2) If I should be in an irreversible coma or persistent vegetative state, or other permanent unconscious condition as certified by two physicians, and from which those physicians believe that I have no reasonable probability of recovery, I direct that life-sustaining treatment be withheld or withdrawn.

3) If I am diagnosed to be in a terminal or permanent unconscious condition (check and initial one only)

_____ I WANT

_____ I DO NOT WANT

artificially administered nutrition and hydration to be withdrawn or withheld the same as other forms of life-sustaining treatment. I understand artificially administered nutrition and hydration is a form of life-sustaining treatment in certain circumstances. I request all health care providers who care for me to honor this directive.[5]

4) In the absence of my ability to give directions regarding the use of such life-sustaining procedures, it is my intention that this directive shall be honored by my family, physicians and other health care providers as the final expression of my fundamental right to refuse medical or surgical treatment, and also honored by any person appointed to make these decisions for me, whether by durable power of attorney or otherwise. I accept the consequences of such refusal.

I understand the full importance of this directive and I am emotionally and mentally competent to make this directive. I also understand that I may amend or revoke this directive at any time.

Signed on _____, _____ (DATE)

_____

NAME

The declarer has been personally known to me and I believe him to be of sound mind. In addition, I am not

---

5   Rose signed a living will when she lived in assisted living and was independent. She wanted to live if not terminable or in an irreversible coma. Rose loved life.

the attending physician, an employee of the attending physician or health care facility in which the declarer is a patient, related to the declarer by blood, marriage or adoption, or a person who has any claim against any portion of the estate of the declarer upon the declarer's decease at the time of the execution of the directive.

SIGNATURE OF WITNESS

_____

Print Name

Signed on _____, _____ (DATE)

SIGNATURE OF WITNESS

_____

Print Name

Signed on _____, _____ (DATE)

2

Durable Power of Attorney Example

Definition: A durable power of attorney is another type of advance directive. It is a document that allows you to name a person as your health care agent to oversee your medical care and make health care decisions for you if you ever become unable to do so at any time. It may also authorize financial decisions to be made for you.

Every state has different laws and requirements for properly executing a durable power of attorney document. Please check to find out what your state requires. This is an example of a durable power of attorney required to be signed by Rose at the "skilled" nursing facility.

ROSE, (hereinafter "the Principal") the undersigned individual, domiciled and residing in the State of _____, designates the following persons as Attorney-in-Fact to act for her, who may hereafter become disabled or incompetent.

1. Designation.

   KELLY, her son, or KAROL, her daughter, are designated as Attorney-in-Fact for ROSE. Either may act for any decision that does not involve health care for ROSE. For health care decisions, both must act together.

2. Powers.

A. General Powers. The Attorney-in-Fact, as fiduciary, shall have all powers of an absolute owner over the assets and liabilities of the Principal, whether located within or without the State of _____. Without limiting the powers herein, the Attorney-in-Fact shall have full power, right and authority to sell, lease, rent, exchange, and otherwise deal with any and all property, real or personal, belonging to the Principal the same as if he/she were the absolute owner thereof. In addition, the Attorney-in-Fact shall have specific powers including, but not limited to the following:

   a) "Skilled" nursing. The Attorney-in-Fact shall have authority to make decisions for Rose during her stay and residence at "skilled" nursing in _____; and in particular in the selection of her room.[6]

   b) Personal Property. The Attorney-in-Fact shall have authority to purchase, receive, take possession

---

6　This was a particular power Rose requested be in her Durable Power at the "skilled" nursing facility.

of, lease, sell, assign, endorse, exchange, release, mortgage and pledge personal property or any interest in personal property.

c) Claims Against the Principal. The Attorney-in-Fact shall have authority to pay, settle, compromise or otherwise discharge any and all claims of liability or indebtedness against the Principal and, in so doing, use any of the assets of the Attorney-in-Fact and obtain reimbursement out of the Principal's funds or other assets.

d) Financial Accounts. The Attorney-in-Fact shall have the authority to deal with accounts maintained by or on behalf of the Principal with institutions (including, without limitation, banks, savings and loan associations, credit unions and securities dealers). This shall include the authority to maintain and close existing accounts, to open, maintain and close other accounts and to make deposits and withdrawals with respect to all such accounts.

e) Legal Proceedings. The Attorney-in-Fact shall have authority to participate in any legal action in the name of the Principal or otherwise.

B. Gifting Power. The Attorney-in-Fact shall have the power to make any gifts, whether outright or in trust, during the Principal's lifetime which are consistent with the most current Will executed by or on behalf of the Principal.

C. Health Care Decisions.[7]

a) General Statement of Authority Granted. The Attorney-in-Fact shall have full power and authority to make health care decisions for the Principal to the same extent that the Principal could make such decisions for the Principal if the Principal had the capacity to do so. In exercising this authority, the Attorney-in-Fact shall make health care decisions that are consistent with the Principal's desires as stated in this document or otherwise made known to the Attorney-in-Fact, including, but not limited to, the following:

1) To consent, refuse, or withdraw consent to any and all types of medical care, treatment, surgical procedures, diagnostic procedures, medication, and the use of mechanical or other procedures that affect any bodily function, including, but not limited to, artificial respiration, nutritional support and hydration, and cardiopulmonary resuscitation;

2) To authorize the admission to or discharge from (even if against medical advice) any hospital, nursing home, residential care, assisted living or similar facility or service;

3) To contract on behalf of the Principal for any health care-related service or facility;

4) To hire and fire medical, social service, and

---

7 The Federal Patient Self Determination Act requires Medicare and Medicaid facilities to inform patients of their rights to execute advance directives.

other support personnel responsible for the
care of the Principal;

5) To give the Attorney-In-Fact first priority in
visitation should the Principal be a patient in
any hospital, health care facility, hospice or
institution and should the Principal be unable
to express a preference because of the Principal's illness or disability;

6) To authorize any medicine or procedures
intended to relieve pain, even though such use
may lead to physical damage, addiction, or
hasten the moment of, but not intentionally
cause, the death of the Principal;

7) To make anatomical gifts of part or all of the
Principal's body for medical purposes, authorize an autopsy, and direct the disposition of the
Principal's remains, to the extent permitted by
law;

8) To take possession of all personal property
belonging to the Principal that may be recovered from or about the person of the Principal
at the time the Principal's illness, disability or
death; and

9) To take any other action necessary to do what
is authorized herein, including, but not limited
to, granting any waiver or release from liability required by any hospital, physician, or
other health care provider; signing any documents relating to refusals of treatment or the
leaving of a facility against medical advice, and

pursuing any legal action in the name of the Principal and at the expense of the Principal's estate to force compliance with the Principal's wishes.

b) Inspection and Disclosure of Information Relating to the Principal's Physical and Mental Health. Without limiting the general powers granted in this instrument, the Attorney-in-Fact has the power and authority to do all of the following:

1) Request, review, and receive any information, verbal or written, regarding the Principal's physical or mental health, including, but not limited to, medical and hospital records.

2) Execute, on the Principal's behalf, any releases or other documents that may be required in order to obtain the above information.

3) Consent to the disclosure of the above information.

c) Signing Documents, Waivers, and Releases. Where necessary to implement the health care decisions that the Attorney-in-Fact is authorized by this document to make, the Attorney-in-Fact has the power and authority to exercise and execute, on the Principal's behalf, all of the following:

1) Documents titled or purporting to be a "Refusal to Permit Treatment" and "Leaving Hospital Against Medical Advice."

2) Any necessary waiver or release from liability

required by a hospital, health care facility, or physician.

d) Prior Designations Revoked. This durable power of attorney revokes any prior durable power of attorney for health care executed by the Principal.

3.   Intent to Obviate Need for Guardianship. It is the Principal's intent that the power given to the Attorney-in-Fact designated herein be interpreted to be so broad as to obviate the need for the appointment of a guardian for the person or estate of the Principal. If the appointment of a guardian or limited guardian of the person or estate of the Principal is sought, however, the Principal nominates the then acting Attorney-in-Fact designated above, if any, as the Principal's guardian or limited guardian, or if no one is then acting as Attorney-in-Fact, the Principal nominates the persons designated above as Attorney-in-Fact and successor Attorneys-in-Fact as guardian or limited guardian, in the same order of priority.

4.   Effectiveness. This power of attorney shall become effective immediately and shall continue in effect regardless of the disability or incompetence of the Principal.[8] Disability

---

8   A durable power of attorney can last for years and does not expire or terminate upon the principal's disability or incompetence. A general power

shall include the inability to manage property and personal affairs for reasons such as mental illness, mental deficiency, physical illness or disability, advanced age, confinement, or disappearance.

5. Duration. This power of attorney becomes effective as provided in Paragraph 4 and shall remain in effect to the extent permitted by the laws of the State of _____ or until revoked or terminated under Paragraphs 5 or 6, notwithstanding any uncertainty as to whether the Principal is dead or alive.

6. Revocation. This power of attorney may be revoked, suspended or terminated in writing by the Principal with written notice to the designated Attorney-in-Fact, and if the same has been recorded, then by recording the written instrument of revocation with the Recorder of the county where the power of attorney is recorded.

7. Termination. The death of the Principal shall be deemed to revoke this power of attorney

---

of attorney does terminate in these events. Both types of powers of attorney terminate on the death of the principal (person granting the power). Many people believe that the person holding a power of attorney for another can continue to act after the principal's death. That is not an estate plan that works.

upon actual knowledge or actual notice being received by the Attorney-in-Fact.

8. Accounting. The Attorney-in-Fact shall be required to account to any subsequently appointed personal representative.

9. Reliance. The designated and acting Attorney-in-Fact and all persons dealing with the Attorney-in-Fact shall be entitled to rely upon this Power of Attorney so long as neither the Attorney-in-Fact nor any person with whom she/he was dealing at the time of any act taken pursuant to this power of attorney had received actual knowledge or actual notice of any revocation, suspension or termination of the power of attorney by death or otherwise. Any action so taken, unless otherwise invalid or unenforceable, shall be binding on the heirs, devisees, legatees or personal representatives of the Principal. In addition, third parties shall be entitled to rely upon a photocopy of the signed original herein, as opposed to a certified copy of the same.

10. Applicable Law. The laws of the State of_____ shall govern this power of attorney.

11. Execution. This power of attorney is signed on this 12th day of November 2005, to

become effective as provided in Paragraph 4.

_____

ROSE _____

STATE OF _____)

) ss.

COUNTY OF _____)

On the 12th day of November 2005, before me, _____ personally appeared ROSE_____. Personally known to me, or proved to me on the basis of satisfactory evidence to be the person whose name is subscribed to the within instrument and acknowledged to me that she executed the same in her authorized capacity, and that by her signature on the instrument theperson, or the entity upon behalf of which the person acted, executed the instrument.

Witness my hand and official seal.

_____

NOTARY PUBLIC in and for the State of _____, residing at _____. Commission Expires _____

3

Physician's Order for Life-Sustaining Treatment

Definition: A Physician Order for Life-Sustaining Treatment (POLST) form can be used by any adult, 18 years of age or older, with serious health conditions. The POLST form is portable from one care setting to another and its intent is to communicate the wishes of an individual into actual medical orders. The form works even if you later lose the ability to speak for yourself. The POLST Form gives medical orders to emergency health care professionals to follow. An advance directive, such as a living will or durable power of attorney, is a legal document, not a medical order, and does not provide treatment orders.

The POLST originated in Oregon in 1991. It quickly spread to other states. POLST is known by different names in different states. In 2004, the National POLST Task Force was started. The Board of Directors is comprised of one representative chosen by each state that has a program.

The National POLST Program is intended to help persons get the medical treatments they want when they are seriously ill or frail. Go to http://POLST.org for more information that may be helpful for you. There are links to state-specific POLST forms online in the resource library of the National POLST Paradigm Task Force at www.POLST.org/educational-resources/resource-library; select "Forms" under "Resource type."

A POLST is a straightforward two-sided form. It can vary somewhat from state to state in the way it is organized.

You may use a POLST to choose clear and specific medical orders that indicate what types of life-sustaining treatment you want or do not want *at the end of life*. This is very serious. These are your instructions for the end of your life. An attending physician, an ARNP (an advanced registered nurse practitioner) or a PA-C (certified physician assistant) must sign the form and assume full responsibility for its accuracy. Education requirements vary greatly among a physician, ARNP, and PA-C.

You must be careful that a POLST form is signed by someone who truly is qualified, and not just by their credentials. It should be someone caring who seriously discusses with you your end-of-life choices, and who is there to help you and your loved one make the type of decisions required on a POLST. No witnessing or notarizing is required.

A POLST can mean life or death. If not done correctly or proper POLST procedures are not followed, the POLST can be your worst enemy. Because the law regulating a POLST varies from state to state and is still developing, there can be errors made in following POLST procedures.

POLST forms are generally organized as follows:

Section A: Cardiopulmonary Resuscitation (CPR)

Section A applies only when the person is unresponsive, has no pulse and is not breathing. The POLST allows people to indicate if they want CPR, unlike a Do-Not-Resuscitate Order when no CPR is desired.

Section B: Medical Interventions

Section B gives the medical orders when CPR is not required but the person has a medical emergency and cannot communicate. For instance, if the person has had a stroke, he or she may not be able to communicate. There are three options and room for specific orders desired by the person. This tells emergency personnel what treatments the person wants. These critical choices are:

Full Treatment. To provide all treatments necessary (and medically appropriate) to keep the person alive. In a medical emergency, the person wants to go to the hospital and, if necessary, be put in the intensive care unit (ICU) and on a breathing machine.

Limited Treatment/Select Treatment. To provide basic medical treatments. The person wants to go to the hospital but does not want to be put in the intensive care unit (ICU) or on a breathing machine. Antibiotics and IV fluids are OK.

Comfort Measures Only. This choice is to make the person as comfortable as possible where he or she is. The person does not want to go to the hospital. If comfort cannot be provided where they are, a transfer to the hospital may be necessary.

These Section B details are important. When people experience a medical emergency, these decisions can save lives when properly applied. Do not take them lightly.

Section C:

This is where the physician or other authorized medical personnel signs and dates the POLST form with the person or his/her legal representative (person designated as the durable power of attorney for health care or a legal guardian). *If signed by the legal representative, the person must be incapacitated to make these decisions.*[9]

A copy of any advance care directive such as a durable power of attorney for health care or a living

---

9 An inexperienced or uncaring authorized medical person may choose to have a person's durable power of attorney holder sign the POLST because it is easier or quicker to explain to that person and less personal, rather than taking the time to go through the decisions and choices that the actual person impacted by the POLST needs to make. Be careful with this.

will should be kept with the POLST. If there is a conflict between the documents, *the most recent takes precedence.*[10]

Section D:

This. provides for Additional Personal Preferences: 1. Should Antibiotics be used? 2. Should Medically Assisted Nutrition be Used? Trial period or Long Term if offering food and liquids by mouth is not feasible?

The back of the form after Section D. also gives contact information, additional directions on the use of the POLST, and a section for review of the POLST form.

The review is critical and can be fatal to a person if a review is not conducted.

The POLST should be reviewed and discussed whenever: 1. There is a transfer from one care setting or care level to another, such as a hospital or "skilled" nursing facility, 2. There is a substantial change in the person's health status, or 3. The person's treatment preferences change.

A person with capacity or the legal representative of a person who lacks capacity can void the form

---

10   The POLST may be the last document signed by a person. People may not remember they signed a POLST and made choices years before about the end of their life. It is absolutely critical that a POLST be reviewed and updated and not left in a file by a "skilled" nursing facility or other medical care provider. The POLST can mean life or death for a person depending on others to follow correct POLST guidelines. POLST forms do not expire. Persons may be held to choices made many years before and, at the actual end of life, their preferences may have changed.

and request alternative treatment.[11] That's why it is so important a POLST is kept current. The health care provider is supposed to go over the POLST form with the person or his or her legal representative when one of these three events occurs. However, these are guidelines, not laws. That is why you have to be diligent in making sure POLST procedures are followed at all times. There is a very good chance that many "skilled" nursing facilities do not train their staff and these procedures will not be followed. If asked under oath if they did follow POLST procedures, they will likely lie and say yes.

The POLST when properly used, it is intended to be an approach to end-of-life planning based on meaningful conversations among the person, loved ones, and medical professionals.[12] To complete the POLST correctly and keep it current, there must be a discussion of the person/person's diagnosis and prognosis; the available treatment options given the current circumstances, including the benefits and burdens of those treatments; and the person's goals of care and preferences of treatment.[13] This type of discussion is the only way to reach an informed decision about desired treatments, based on the person's values, beliefs and goals for care at that

---

11   We would have wanted Full Treatment for Rose. That is what she wanted. She wanted to live. That is not what "skilled" nursing gave her.

12   We were never told by any medical care provider that Rose was in an end-of-life condition. She wanted to live, and we wanted her to live. They hid the truth about the mistakes they made that led to her death.

13   Not one medical care provider had any type of discussion with Rose, my brother, or me about her real condition and the choices we had to save her. They hid the truth knowing she would die.

time. The POLST must be kept current. It is not a form to fill out only once. When a medical emergency or condition occurs, that can mean the end of life. Affect people and their loved ones have a right to understand and know what the choices are.

A POLST must be easily modified or revoked. A person's preferences for certain treatments may change over time. As a person's health changes over time, his/ her goals of care may change.[14]

A POLST form is intended to be easily located in an emergency. Advance directive documents are generally at home or in a lawyer's office and not readily available to emergency medical personnel.

Persons with decision-making capacity can modify their POLST at any time to reflect changing

---

14 As an example, Rose signed a POLST in 2009 that was then placed in her file at the "skilled" nursing facility. She completed it with an ARNP, who was later fired for inappropriate and incompetent handling of residents. The "skilled" nursing facility never updated the POLST. No one in the facility ever had a discussion with Rose or her designated family members for her durable power of attorney for health care. Rose went to the hospital and back to "skilled" nursing in 2010 and 2011. You may remember in Part One that Rose was treated with good results at the hospital before her last stay in 2012. The "skilled" nursing facility never updated the 2009 POLST after the 2010 and 2011 hospital stays. Rose's treatment preferences had changed significantly after her hospital stays and good results. Rose wanted to live and wanted help. Rose had her medical emergency or "change in condition" in 2012. The "skilled" nursing never informed us there was an old POLST in her file. If they had followed POLST guidelines, the POLST would have been reviewed and brought current after the 2010 and 2011 hospital stays and especially in 2012 when Rose had a change in condition. Rose could have survived if the POLST had been followed correctly. The "skilled" nursing was incompetent and people there did not tell the truth under penalty of perjury later in a nursing investigation. See access to medical records in Part Two.

circumstances. As an example, a stroke is less serious and disabling than once feared. Treatment may have been initiated and once more medical information becomes available regarding diagnosis, prognosis, or potential outcomes, the person's goals and preferences may change. If the person becomes incapacitated, the advance directive plays an important role in developing goals for care consistent with the person in his/her new state of health. The legal representative identified by the person in his/her advance directive would participate in either initiating a POLST or updating POLST orders in a manner consistent with the person's preferences as the person's health status changes.

The POLST form is not intended to replace an advance directive document or other medical orders. The two documents differ, but they ideally work together. In short, the POLST turns the person's wishes expressed in an advance directive into action as a medical order.

4

Abuse of Vulnerable Adult Statute

Abuse, neglect, and fraud to the elderly and vulnerable adults is a growing problem across the U.S. as the population ages. This can be physical or psychological abuse, neglect, and/or financial fraud. Federal and state laws vary in the definition of these terms. These are under reported crimes. Many cases are never prosecuted and brought to justice. Even if reported, the time lag between the event and the trial date can be so long that any effective punishment is negated.

In the late 1980s, the National Center on Elder Abuse (NCEA) was formed, but any attempts in the U.S. Congress to pass any elder abuse acts have all failed. Any remedy for the elderly or vulnerable adults relies on each state to pass protective laws.

Many states have enacted statutes to protect elderly and vulnerable adults residents of nursing homes and other health care facilities or services such as home health care. In the case of nursing homes, these statutes have helped to counteract the power imbalance

between helpless elderly residents and powerful corporate-owned nursing homes.

Civil Actions

In addition to the criminal and administrative
protections for vulnerable adults, most state statutes
provide for civil actions for damages based on the
neglect, abandonment, abuse, or financial exploitation
of vulnerable persons. Also included are attorneys' fees
and costs to a prevailing plaintiff as added incentive
for plaintiffs' attorneys to pursue damages on behalf
of people in the last years of their lives. Some states
even provide for punitive damages, which can help
an injured elder or vulnerable adult find a lawyer and
recover something to compensate them for all their
suffering.

As an example, in 1991, California enacted the
Elder Abuse and Dependent Protection Act to protect
vulnerable and elderly adults. Under California law,
vulnerable adults and elderly victims of abuse are
entitled to: compensatory damages, pain and suffering
damages, punitive damages, attorney's fees and equitable relief. Arizona and Florida also provide for punitive
damages. Be sure to check and see what states have
punitive damages that may be connected to your Vulnerable Adults Statutes (VAS) claim.

As people grow older, the economic value of their
lives declines for calculating damages in a lawsuit.
That is why so many law firms have not been interested in pursuing lawsuits against nursing homes. A

study by insurance companies showed that the average settlement or recovery in a nursing home lawsuit was $30,000–$40,000.[15] That low pay=off amount has allowed nursing homes to get by with abuse and or murder.

Change the Playing Field

The Vulnerable Adults Statutes as enacted by most states across the country have helped to change the playing field. The cards are still stacked in the favor of the nursing homes, but the VAS brought an opportunity for justice for those elderly and vulnerable adults injured.

In one state, as an example, a vulnerable adult is a resident in a Department of Social and Health Services (DSHS) licensed facility or a person who receives home health care from DSHS licensed individuals.[16] "Facilities" are nursing homes, boarding homes, adult family homes, soldiers' homes, residential habilitation centers, and any other facility licensed by DSHS.

A vulnerable adult must meet one or any combination of the criteria that follow:

1) 60 years of age or older who has the functional, mental, or physical inability to care for himself or herself, or

---

15   https://aspe.hhs.gov/basic-report/recent-trends-nursing-home-liability-insurance-market

16   Code Chapter 74.34

2) Found incapacitated under the guardianship statute, or

3) Is developmentally disabled, or

4) Admitted to any DSHS licensed facility, or

5) Receiving services from home health, hospice, or home care agencies licensed or required to be licensed, or

6) Receiving services from an individual provider who is under contract by DSHS.

The civil action survives the death of a vulnerable adult. The executor or administrator of the deceased's estate may recover all damages for the benefit of the deceased person's statutory beneficiaries or, if there are no statutory beneficiaries, economic damages may be recovered for the deceased person's estate.

Definition

The word "abuse" suggests an overt physical act. However, under the Abuse of Vulnerable Adults Statute, **simple neglect that causes injuries, pain, and suffering,** and loss of property is actionable abuse. **Abandonment, abuse, financial exploitation, and neglect** are all bases for a lawsuit. Neglect is most often used as the basis for a lawsuit; when there is neglect, there's often an abandonment claim. A nursing home that neglects to provide adequate nutrition or health care to a vulnerable adult is liable under the statute for abandonment as well as leaving a person without the means or ability to obtain necessary food, clothing, shelter, or health care.

"Neglect" under the statute has two alternative definitions. First, neglect is "a pattern of conduct or inaction by a person or entity with a duty of care that fails to provide the goods and services that maintain physical or mental health of a vulnerable adult, or that fails to avoid or prevent physical or mental harm or pain to a vulnerable adult."

Or second, neglect is "an act or omission that demonstrates a serious disregard of consequences of such a magnitude as to constitute a clear and present danger to the vulnerable adult's health, welfare, or safety."[17]

Under the first definition of neglect, the plaintiff must prove that the defendant engaged in a pattern of conduct or inaction. The statute does not define what establishes a pattern and over what time course the conduct or inaction must occur.

Proving a pattern of conduct or inaction has not been difficult in nursing home cases. Most nursing home neglect cases will result from multiple acts or omissions. Each day, a resident is cared for by three shifts of nurses and nursing assistants. The resident who continues to be dehydrated or malnourished is

---

17 Roger J. Leslie. Trial News. *Washington State Association for Justice*, February 2011, Volume: 46-6.

neglected three times a day, which establishes a pattern of conduct or inaction.

The second type of neglect involves an act or omission that constitutes a clear and present danger to the vulnerable adult. Usually, a finding of an act or omission by a person with a duty of care for a dependent person that creates a clear and present danger to the vulnerable adult will fulfill the "serious disregard of consequences" element of the statutory neglect.

Neglect under the VAS is not the same as the common law tort of negligence.

It is generally more difficult for a plaintiff to prevail in a medical negligence claim than in a claim against a nursing home corporation that has created a danger to residents by under staffing the facility and by under training the staff.

Another issue for a VAS claim is if the medical director for a nursing home provides negligent care. A nursing home that received funds from Medicare and Medicaid must provide a licensed physician as its medical director. Medical directors may choose to call themselves independent contractors to a nursing home, but in many cases they satisfy the factors that prove either an actual or apparent agency relationship. "Neglect" is easier to show and prove than "medical negligence," which has different standards. The medical director, partners physicians, and the associated medical clinic will fight tooth and nail with their insurance lawyers to counter any medical negligence claim. These are tough cases before a jury, which generally does not like to find against a local doctor. The cards are stacked against you in these fights.

Value of Life Under the Law

The older you are, the less value your life has under the laws of the United States. All those years of experiences and knowledge are ready to be thrown out in a courtroom. Personal injuries lawyers generally are not interested in cases that involve an injury or death of an older person. That's because these types of cases generally are done on a contingency basis, and a percentage of a small life value does not pay much.[18]

It is sad but true. The nursing homes can get by hurting residents or even causing their death because they know the actuarial value of that life is not much. What scary stuff as you age and have to trust these caregivers! We trusted the people who took care of Rose. She was always nice to them thinking that they cared about her. They didn't in the end.

Also because of the increase in nursing home litigation, many states enacted "tort" reform to actually limit the amount of a recovery against nursing homes, even when they were found guilty of abuse, neglect, or even wrongful death. Again, the system is tipped against consumers.

---

18   A contingency case is when the law firm advances the expenses and takes a percentage of the settlement or damages awarded in a case. The longer the case goes, the higher the percentage (33-50% typically). Expenses advanced are paid back from the recovery.

Punitive Damages

A few states provide for punitive damages, which does give the inured party a greater chance for a bigger recovery. Punitive damages[19] are designed to punish the nursing home, as they should be in many situations. But if your loved one resides in a state where putative damages are not allowed, you are limited in the damages you can claim, no matter how awful the nursing home's behavior. This was part of the reason that personal injury lawyers lost interest in taking cases for older persons. Small life value and no punitive damages did not leave much room for big case awards and attorney fees.

When the Abuse of Vulnerable Adult statutes were enacted, they helped injured adults and their families find a lawyer. If there is abuse, abandonment, neglect and worst of all wrongful death, the lawyer who takes the case can at least recover hourly time and costs if a settlement or court award is made under the VAS. This encourages lawyers to take these cases. It may not be as big of a recovery as in a personal injury case on a contingency, but it does compensate a lawyer for his or her time.

Litigation against nursing homes began to increase

---

19   Punitive damages may be awarded in addition to actual damages, which compensate a plaintiff for the losses suffered due to the harm caused by the defendant. Punitive damages are a way of punishing the defendant in a civil lawsuit and are based on the theory that the interests of society and the individual harmed can be met by imposing additional damages on the defendant. Since the 1970s, punitive damages have been criticized by U.S. business and insurance groups, which allege that exorbitant punitive damage awards have driven up the cost of doing business.

with the aging population in the 1990s, and the insurance industry began to cut back on insuring nursing homes. Many nursing homes turned to self insurance through a captive insurance pool (a company that a number of businesses contribute to as a pool to share the risk). These are normally not highly funded. That means your chances of recovering damages are lower because there is a smaller insurance pool from which to settle or pay damages.

In Appendix C, you'll find an article published by the Kaiser Health Organization that tells how nursing homes are structured to avoid liability and paying damages, even when there is abuse and wrongful death of residents.

How Can You Protect Yourself and Your Loved Ones?

I give you this advice as a daughter who will forever believe she lost her mother to a wrongful death from nursing home abuse and neglect. This is not legal advice, even though I am a lawyer. I am telling you like it is and straight from the heart.

First, never sign a contract with a caregiver that requires arbitration. Many nursing home contracts require arbitration and thus block you from suing them in a court of law. Also arbitration awards are generally much smaller than an award in a civil trial with judge or jury. Arbitrators are professionals dealing with negotiation every day. There's no emotion with them as you may have with a jury.

In 2016, the Centers for Medicaid and Medicare Service passed a rule that would ban nursing homes and assisted living facilities from forcing patients and their families into private arbitration to resolve any disputes. The rule was not put into place in 2017. Court challenges by the nursing home and healthcare industry have kept it on hold. This is very important to watch. Forced arbitration gives the injured party very little in leverage and keeps the bad nursing home hidden from the public. That's what the nursing homes want, to keep their bad behavior buried.

Second, right from the start, make it clear that you want and have current access to the medical records. Records may be hidden, destroyed, or missing if you go back after an injury or a death and ask to get them. You have a right at all times to review medical records and get copies. Don't let them tell you otherwise. If they don't want you to see the records, that is a bad sign.

If there is a death, make sure you get an autopsy. (Read more about this in Part Two: Chapter 7: The Importance of an Autopsy.) Rose's death was a cover up, yet we couldn't nail them with her death because we didn't think fast enough to get an autopsy. It would have shown they caused her death. Instead, all we had was her death certificate and cause of death listed by the medical director for "skilled" nursing.

Third, if you are fortunate to find a good lawyer as we did, be thankful. Many lawyers are not interested in helping you unless it will be an easy case with a big payoff for them. Even with the VAS, we found that lawyers still want the easy case with the best facts: younger person, autopsy, nursing home with good insurance, nursing home management, operation or ownership located in a state that has punitive damages, records in order, health department or DSHS investigations competent and honest, and not too much time has passed (three-year statute of limitations to file a claim against the nursing home in most cases).

5

An Elder Abuse and Wrongful Death Lawsuit Example

Example Lawsuit using Rose as the Injured Party

Plaintiff, by and through undersigned counsel, for her causes of action against Defendant, alleges as follows:

I. PARTIES; JURISDICTION; VENUE

1. Plaintiff, Daughter, a resident of a County, in a State, and is the duly appointed personal representative of the Estate of Rose, and by order of the Superior Court of a County is authorized to commence and maintain this action on behalf of the Estate of Rose and the statutory beneficiaries, Rose's daughter and son.

2. Defendant "skilled" nursing at all times material hereto engaged in the business of operating a nursing home.

3.   All acts and omissions alleged herein occurred in County, and venue is proper in County.

4.   NOTE; DEFENDANTS DENIED EVEN THESE BASIC TRUE FACTS IN I.

II. FACTS GIVING RISE TO LIABILITY

5.   "Skilled" nursing held out its facility to the public as a nursing facility, "skilled" in the performance of nursing and other medical support services, and as being properly equipped and staffed to care for residents in need of nursing and medical care.

6.   On November 2, 2005, Rose was admitted to "skilled" nursing.

7.   In exchange for valuable consideration, "skilled" nursing undertook to furnish Rose with room and board and to provide necessary medical attention and care which she might require while a resident at "skilled" nursing.

8.   On the morning of August 16, 2012 ...

Note: Facts 9 through 20 are omitted to protect the guilty as required by a settlement forced on the family of Rose.

21. Rose's death was the result of careless and improper care by "skilled" nursing entire staff.

III. CAUSES OF ACTION
COUNT I (GENERAL NEGLIGENCE)

22. Plaintiff realleges paragraphs 1 through 21 above.

23. "Skilled" nursing had a duty to exercise the degree of care expected of a reasonably prudent nursing home facility and a duty to safeguard Rose's condition and well-being.

24. "Skilled" nursing failed to exercise the degree of care expected of a reasonably prudent nursing home facility acting in similar circumstances.

25. Among other acts and omissions, "skilled" nursing and its employees:

1) failed to train and supervise properly its employees with respect to safeguarding and monitoring the physical condition and well-being of its residents including Rose;

2) failed to monitor Rose's condition and well-being;

3) failed to adequately diagnose and treat the left frontal lacunar ischemic stroke, or transfer Rose if they could not diagnose or treat it;

4) failed to develop and implement an adequate plan of care for Rose; and

5) failed to provide adequate nursing care to Rose.

26. As a result of "skilled" nursing's acts and omissions, Rose suffered severe, debilitating, and ultimately fatal harm.

COUNT II (RESPONDEAT SUPERIOR)

27. Plaintiff realleges paragraphs 1 through 26 above.

28. "Skilled" nursing's failure to exercise the appropriate degree of care was a proximate cause of injuries to Rose, including pain and suffering, resulting in her death.

29. "Skilled" nursing is vicariously liable for the conduct of their employees in the course and scope of employment.

COUNT III (NEGLIGENT SUPERVISION AND RETENTION)

30. Plaintiff realleges paragraphs 1 through 29 above.

31. "Skilled" nursing had a duty to train and supervise its employees to ensure that competent nursing care was provided to Rose.

32. "Skilled" nursing breached its duty because the it knew or should have known that the nursing staff was understaffed, incompetent, improperly trained, and/or poorly supervised.

33. "Skilled" nursing acted negligently in hiring, supervising, and retaining its nursing staff and employees.

34. As a result of such conduct, Rose suffered severe injuries, pain and suffering, resulting in her death.

COUNT IV (BREACH OF CONTRACT)

35. Plaintiff realleges paragraphs 1 through 34 above.

36. On information and belief, on or about November 2, 2005, Rose and Karol entered into a contract with "skilled" nursing whereby "skilled" nursing agreed to provide all due and proper care for Rose's condition and well-being and agreed to provide necessary medical care.

37. Rose at all times performed in accordance with the terms of the contract.

38. "Skilled" nursing failed to safeguard Rose's condition and well-being and failed to provide her with proper care, in breach of contract.

39. As a result of such conduct, Rose suffered severe injuries and pain and suffering, resulting in her death.

COUNT V (VIOLATION OF STATUTES)

40. Plaintiff realleges paragraphs 1 through 39 above.

41. The laws of the State of _____ include numerous provisions designed to maintain the appropriate level of care of residents in nursing homes in State.

42. "Skilled" nursing's care of Rose was regulated by state law and regulations set forth, *inter alia*, in the Revised Code of State and the State Administrative Code.

43. Among other violations of the applicable laws and regulations, "skilled" nursing failed to treat Rose with consideration, respect, and full recognition of her dignity, in violation of CODE 74.42.050 and CODE 388-97-0860, among other statutes and regulations.

44. "Skilled" nursing failed to provide appropriate medical services and nursing care in violation of CODE 74.42.140, CODE 74.42.160, CODE 388-97-0020, CODE 388-97-1000, CODE 388-97-1060, CODE 388-97-1080, CODE 388-97-1260,

and CODE 388-97-1640, among other statutes and regulations.

45. As a result of "skilled" nursing's violations of law, including but not limited to the provisions set forth above, "skilled" nursing caused harm to Rose, resulting in her death.

46. Plaintiff realleges paragraphs 1 through 45 above.

47. "Skilled" nursing's acts and omissions constitute extreme and outrageous conduct.

48. "Skilled" nursing and its employees inflicted pain and suffering and emotional distress on Rose prior to her death.

49. As a result of "skilled" nursing's violations of law, including but not limited to the provisions set forth above, "skilled" nursing caused harm to Rose.

COUNT VII (COMMON LAW FRAUD)

50. Plaintiff realleges paragraphs 1 through 49 above.

51. The acts and representations of "skilled" nursing constitute common law fraud.

52. "Skilled" nursing, with intent to defraud Rose,

represented that they would provide a well-trained and competent nursing staff to provide proper care for her.

53. These representations were false and known to be false by "skilled" nursing at the time they were made.

54. In fact, "skilled" nursing was aware that the nursing staff was often understaffed and not properly trained.

55. Rose was ignorant of the falsity of the representations and believed them to be true.

56. Relying on the representations, Rose entered into a contract with "skilled" nursing and became a resident of "skilled" nursing.

57. "Skilled" nursing made the representations for the purpose of inducing Rose to accept their services.

58. As a result of "skilled" nursing's fraud, Rose was seriously injured and died.

COUNT VIII (NEGLIGENT MISREPRESENTATION)

59. Plaintiff re-alleges paragraphs 1 through 58 above.

60. "Skilled" nursing represented that they would provide adequate nursing care to Rose. "skilled" nursing knew or should have known that their representations were false.

61. The acts and representations of "skilled" nursing constitute negligent misrepresentation.

62. As a result of such conduct, Rose suffered severe injuries and pain and suffering, resulting in her death.

COUNT IX (LOSS OF CHANCE)

63. Plaintiff realleges paragraphs 1 through 62 above.

64. The actions of "skilled" nursing reduced Rose's chance of recovery and as a direct result of "skilled" nursing's actions, Rose suffered severe injuries and died.

COUNT IX (ABUSE OF VULNERABLE ADULT)

65. Plaintiff realleges paragraphs 1 through 64 above.

66. "Skilled" nursing failed to safeguard Rose's condition and well-being, failed to provide her with proper care, and subjected her to neglect.

67. "Skilled" nursing's acts and omissions constitute

abandonment, abuse, and neglect of a vulnerable adult.

68. As a result of such conduct, Rose suffered severe injuries and pain and suffering, resulting in her death.

69. Pursuant to CODE 74.34.200, plaintiff is entitled to damages, together with the costs of suit, including reasonable attorney's fees.

COUNT X (WRONGFUL DEATH OF PARENT AND SPOUSE, AND LOSS OF CONSORTIUM, CODE 4.20.010, 4.20.020)

70. Plaintiff realleges paragraphs 1 through 69 above.

71. As a direct and proximate result of the acts and omissions of "skilled" nursing, Rose suffered and died, causing the statutory beneficiaries to sustain damages for funeral expenses, burial expenses, medical expenses, loss of decedent's love, affection, companionship, care, society, guidance, and consortium, including damages for destruction of the parent-child relationship.

COUNT XI (PURSUANT TO CODE 4.20.046, 4.20.060; SURVIVAL ACTION)

72. Plaintiff re-alleges paragraphs 1 through 71 above.

73. As a result of "skilled" nursing's acts and omissions, decedent Rose suffered injuries that caused her death. As a result of "skilled" nursing's acts and omissions, she experienced physical and mental pain, anxiety, distress, shock, humiliation, agony, and suffering, all to her damage in an amount to be proven at the time of trial.

74. In addition, decedent's death resulted in damages for loss of enjoyment of life and general damages.

75. The statutory beneficiaries and the estate of Rose sustained damages as a result of her death pursuant to CODE 4.20.010, 4.20.020, 4.20.046, and 4.20.060.

Note: Don't be surprised when you read below and see how the defendant ("skilled" nursing) answers and denies everything. It is sickening. Here are their actual replies:

In answer to the above question, this defendant denies the same.

FIRST AFFIRMATIVE DEFENSE
Plaintiffs have failed to state a claim upon which relief can be granted.

SECOND AFFIRMATIVE DEFENSE
The care and services provided to Rose "skilled"

nursing do not constitute negligence, including negligence for a survival action, neglect, abuse, fraud, outrage, negligent supervision, breach of contract, violation of statutes, loss of chance, negligent misrepresentation, or wrongful death.

THIRD AFFIRMATIVE DEFENSE
Plaintiffs claim no damage attributable to the claim for Counts II, III, IV, V, VI, VII, VIII, IX, IX, or X that is not also claimed as a damage under plaintiffs' claim for negligence under Count I. Plaintiffs are not entitled to double recovery or multiple recoveries for the same alleged harm.

FOURTH AFFIRMATIVE DEFENSE
Plaintiffs' injuries, if any, may have been caused or contributed to by others over whom defendant has no control or authority, including plaintiffs. Discovery is continuing.

FIFTH AFFIRMATIVE DEFENSE
Plaintiffs had a duty to mitigate their damages. To the extent the evidence establishes that they failed to do so, their damages may be reduced or barred in like kind.

SIXTH AFFIRMATIVE DEFENSE
In the event of an award for future economic damages meeting the threshold, notice is hereby given to plaintiff of the intent to invoke the provisions of CODE 4.56.260.

SEVENTH AFFIRMATIVE DEFENSE
Defendant is entitled to a credit, offset, and/or set-off for payments made.

EIGHTH AFFIRMATIVE DEFENSE
Plaintiffs' claims lack a basis in law and/or fact.

NINTH AFFIRMATIVE DEFENSE
To the extent plaintiffs seek recovery of any damages for medical expenses, the same must be limited to the amount paid, rather than the amount billed, pursuant to controlling State law.

WHEREFORE, having fully answered Plaintiffs' Complaint and having asserted affirmative defenses, this answering defendant prays for the following relief:

1. Plaintiffs' Complaint be dismissed and take nothing thereby;

2. Recovery of allowable attorneys' fees and costs pursuant to state statute and/or court rule;

3. Such other and further relief as the court deems just and equitable.

End of Example Lawsuit

The lawyers for the insurance company for the nursing home do everything they can to intimidate you and hope you will back down. They scare you that you have to pay their fees and costs! When you don't back down, then they stall and lie to you that they are negotiating with their client how much the nursing home is willing to pay you. That is a technique to drag the case out for years. Don't believe them.

6

Access to Medical Records

You may recall from Part One about several lawyers who helped me along the way. Their assistance came without a financial gain to them, and I am forever grateful. These lawyers helped me with the recovery and advancement of necessary papers to keep Mom's death from being swept under the rug. That's what the "skilled" nursing home wanted in the Cover Up. One lawyer helped me get the medical records from "skilled" nursing. The people in charge resisted as much and as long as they could. Another lawyer advised me to get the hospital records too. The hospital complied quickly, and revealing a host of valuable information in those records relevant to the actions or inactions of "skilled" nursing and its medical director.

Together with these records, a better picture developed of what happened to Rose. Another lawyer did the probate filing to have me appointed as Executrix (see Appendix D for an explanation of this important role) so a case could be pursued. The hero of them all was the lawyer who took the case and put in many hours of work organizing the case, the records, and the discovery process.[20]

It was a long, painful process because so many people doubted that something had really happened to Mom. People thought I was not getting over it, that I needed grief counseling, which was insulting to me. It's because they didn't care about Mom. I did, and I knew something was wrong. The "skilled" nursing covered it up so well, it was like looking for the needle in a hay stack. But I knew it was there. I did not give up. You can never give up when you know there has been a wrongful death.

Three-Year Statute of Limitations

From 2012 when we lost Rose, it took almost two-and-a-half years to get all the records. That gave those guilty lots of time to stall, hide, lie, and destroy. There is only a three-year period in most states, called the statute of limitations, in which you must act and file your lawsuit after a wrongful death or VAS violation. We had only three years after August of 2012 to file our complaint.

That's why it is important for you to know exactly what you need to do—and quickly—when something even begins to happen to someone you love. Every

---

20 Discovery in a civil case is a pre-trial procedure in which each party can obtain evidence from the other party or parties by means of discovery devices such as a request for answers to interrogatories, request for production of documents, request for admissions and depositions.

hour and day that goes by, the odds stack against you uncovering the truth.

Because my brother and I trusted the caregivers for Rose, we let our guard down. We trusted to the very end the nurses and doctors who all failed her. It was only when she was gone for no reason and I had that awful call from the "skilled" nursing facility early that morning saying she was gone did I know something was wrong.

She wanted to live. How could she be gone? What did they do to her? Did they end her life quietly in the dark that morning at 5:30? Why did they say to me afterwards, "At least she didn't die alone." Why would they go into her dark room at 5:30 when no one else was around to take a blood draw?

I had been there with her all the day before and had called last thing at night on September 3, 2012, to make sure she was okay. They said they had called the doctor for any orders and that she was breathing calmly. And then the next morning, on September 4, 2012, she was gone!

I believe she could have lived if they had not hurt her and started the Cover Up. If they had been truthful with us, Rose would have lived. I fear they ended her life that early morning in the dark. And then they had the mortuary come and get her body before anyone was awake to witness that Rose had died. In fact, they told me there was no reason to come over then.

I was shocked, and I sobbed and sobbed. I called

my brother and he broke down in tears, too. He said, "She was a fighter."

We were both in shock and not thinking clearly about what had just happened. When we went to the mortuary that afternoon, they never asked if we wanted an autopsy. Rose was cremated as she wanted. The funeral home didn't even put the label on her cremation box on straight—a last insult for poor Mom.

I knew something was wrong. I acted as fast as I could to find the guilty parties responsible for her death. Three days after Rose left us, I filed a complaint with the Department of Health that regulates nurses in nursing homes. They in turn contacted DSHS, a process that's similar in every state. I blamed all the RNs and staff who had failed her, not just one. An investigation, therefore, was against the "unknowns."

All of the "unknowns"—RNs, nursing staff, and head of nursing—were questioned by the Department of Health investigators. None of them told the truth. To me, the investigation was a joke. Each of these "unknowns" was given a letter informing her that a complaint had been filed "alleging" unprofessional conduct by unknown nurses at "skilled" nursing. They were each asked to give a written statement addressing certain "allegations." There was no time constraint or requirement that their statement be answered in any legal setting; they could fill it out at home or anywhere. Of course, they were all to complete the answers and sign under penalty of perjury. Well, can't you just imagine each of these nurses getting a letter like that and being given the chance to discuss it together, fill it out, and sign it when and where they pleased!

Each was asked to respond to the same three questions about how they cared for Rose. The questions were:

1. It is alleged that you failed to assess a patient for a change of condition (defined as health care information readily identifiable to the patient);
2. It is alleged that you failed to notify the family or durable power of attorney of a change in condition of the patient, and
3. It is alleged that you failed to follow the POLST.

All of them signed under penalty of perjury and gave answers that made them look like they did everything 100% correct. Yet any idiot would have known how to best answer those obvious questions to protect themselves.

It made me mad to read their replies. I knew their answers weren't true. They blamed our family in their answers.

Keep a Log

Beware. This could be something to expect if you fight a nursing home. "It's not their fault; it's the family's fault." So prepare yourself for that ahead of time. Catch them in their own lies by being extremely diligent and keeping a log yourself of each day you interact with them.

Their lawyer in the lawsuit asked me if I kept my own diary or log (and it must be kept contemporaneously to be used later in a legal matter). Unfortunately, I did not have my own log in writing. It was only in my head.

I believe the investigation conducted wasn't credible because those at the "skilled" nursing facility didn't tell the truth. They hid records and made declarations under penalty of perjury that were not true. One of the investigators said to me, "It's really hard to catch them after your mom's death. If we can see the problem, we have a chance to fix it. Someone sitting in their wheelchair in a dirty diaper, that's what we are good at catching."

As discussed in the chapter on POLST, Rose's POLST was more than four years old and not current with her wishes for health care at all. They never told us they had an old POLST on file. They never went over it with Rose or with us when she had a "change of condition," as they claim they discussed with us. They never updated it when she left "skilled" nursing in 2010 and 2011 for the hospital and came back. And yet they lied and got by with it in the nursing and DSHS investigation.

Do you see how easy it is to mislead an investigator if the resident has died and records are hidden?

Telling the resident and family about a change of

condition requires the truth, in my view. Although everything they told us was wrong, yet under penalty of perjury they told the investigators they kept the family fully informed. They told Rose, my brother, and me that she had an infection on August 16, and that they could take care of her. They also in detail explained they had called the medical director that morning and he had ordered lab tests right away. Later that day, an antibiotic was ordered.

But Rose didn't have an infection. We know that because the medical director left for a long weekend *before* the lab report came back. No one with any medical knowledge reviewed the lab report. Nevertheless, the nurse practitioner for the medical director's medical clinic ordered an antibiotic for Rose that she did not need.

It was nearly two-and-a-half years later after we lost Rose that I found the truth in all the records from "skilled" nursing and the hospital. Not only had the staff covered up the truth, but so had the medical director and his partners who treated her at the hospital.

Spoliation Laws

Spoliation of evidence laws exist in most states. Spoliation of evidence is the intentional destruction of evidence. This can include the destruction, alteration, tampering, or concealment of physical evidence, and tampering with witnesses. If the caregivers are clever enough and have enough time, it's hard to prove the intent if records go missing. As the insurance lawyers for "skilled" nursing drag out the months and delay the trial, it gives them the time and the edge to cover their tracks and build their defense.

If you file a complaint with the Department of Health, which regulates health care providers, the information will be similar from state to state. Some facilities such as nursing homes and assisted living facilities are regulated by the Department of Social and Health Services (DSHS).

You can also file a complaint with DSHS. Nursing homes are licensed by the Department of Health. So in the case of Rose, when I contacted the Department of Health regarding conduct of the nurses at the "skilled" nursing facility, the officials also contacted DSHS as mentioned earlier.

When a state health department receives a complaint about a healthcare facility, officials review it to decide if the incident or event is a violation of a law or rule. They ask if there is legal authority to investigate the healthcare facility. When these two conditions are met, they open a complaint file, notify the complainant, and conduct an investigation.

Most of the investigations consist of going to the healthcare facility, reviewing patient records, reading and reviewing the facility's policies and procedures, reading and reviewing any facility documents related to the incident, interviewing staff, and depending on the incident, observing staff delivering care. *This means talking to the guilty parties and giving them the opportunity to cover their tracks.* If records are concealed and the injured party has passed away, it's logical to think the investigation will easily fail to uncover the true events.

This process naturally invites the health care regulated nurses to tell their stories the way they want to. The truth does not always come out because they look out for themselves. It's sickening how they can twist the truth.

I wanted to go back and face every one of those nurses and administrators who lied and hold them accountable. I wanted to look them in the eye until they admitted they had lied and caused her death. But that was best done at trial. I wanted the whole incompetent murderous "skilled" nursing home, administrators, nurses, medical director, and staff exposed. That was the point of going to trial.

I appealed the investigation reports because I knew the nurses had lied under penalty of perjury. What they told the investigators and what they told me and my brother about Rose was not the same. The investigators could not find their errors because of this Cover Up.

I also filed an appeal with the state, because "skilled" nursing did not provide all their records in the investigation by the Department of Health. This was nine months after Rose's death. It seemed the "skilled" nursing personnel were doing all they could to delay, hide, and destroy records that were damaging to them.

File an Appeal

If you cannot get complete records from a nursing home, you have to file an appeal with the state department that regulates nurses and nursing homes in your state.

My appeal email chain is in italics below. Remember, Rose left this world unwillingly in September of 2012.

Sent: Tuesday, June_____ 2013
To: (DOH)
Cc: (DSHS/RCS)
Subject: FW: Appeal for Medical Records

Good Day to you:

I am waiting for the medical records from "skilled" nursing for Mom. I have emailed both of you as I think that DHSH might be concerned with what I have seen in the file records sent to me up to this date.

Yesterday I went through the responses the various nurses filed with the nursing commission investigation. It is very disturbing as to the misrepresentations and outright lies about what they did and did not do AND particularly about what they disclosed to "the family" and what the family consented to.

There are things in the file that shocked me. They never told us: 1) that they were following the POLST; they never discussed it with either my brother or me at any stage;

there was no physician discussion with us as I asked for more levels of care and help from them; 2) that they had placed a red flag alert on my Mom; 3) that they considered this an end of life situation. They told us she had an infection and that they could take care of her. To make her better!! Not to end her life !!!

All will be broken down for you. I will write a full analysis of each of the pages submitted by the nursing staff and point out their failures and misrepresentations. They did not inform the family what they were doing. Never did they have a discussion with us about my mom's condition and how to treat it and whether the POLST should be followed. They did not follow POLST procedures at all. To read that they considered this an end of life procedure was shocking to say the least.
Thank you
Karol

-----Original Message-----
From: Karol
Sent: Thursday, June ___, 2013
To: DOH Agency PRR Appeals
Cc: (DOH)
Subject: Appeal for Medical Records

Dear Public Records Officer:
Please find attached letter of Appeal for

records that were withheld from me for my deceased mother, Rose, from the nursing commission investigation of the nurses at "skilled" nursing, a nursing home located at _____. I thank you in advance for your timely response to this very important matter. Yours Truly, Karol

From: DOH Appeals [PRRAppeals@DOH.State. GOV]
Sent: June ___, 2013 10:01 AM
To: Karol
Subject: RE: Appeal for Medical Records

Karol - Please trust that I will step through this as quickly as possible, and I appreciate your willingness to provide additional infor-mation/documentation (should it be needed).
Records Manager & Public Records Officer Office of the Secretary
State Department of Health

From: DOH Agency PRR Appeals [PRRAppeals@ DOH.State.GOV]
Sent: June _____ 2013
To: Karol; DOH Agency PRR Appeals
Cc: (DOH);
Subject: RE: Appeal for Medical Records

Karol – I wanted to let you know that the

*Department acknowledges receipt of your
appeal. I expect that I will be able to complete
my review within a week (assuming contingency planning in the face of a government
shutdown does not take precedence). Should
I determine that additional production is
required by the agency, we'll inform you at
the time of determination when we anticipate
being able to provide those records.*

*Records Manager & Public Records Officer
Office of the Secretary
State Department of Health*

Following this appeal to the top level of the State
for Medical Records, I then had to turn to one of the
few lawyers who did help me. I think he could tell from
my diligence that something was wrong indeed. He frequently wrote about the VAS and he believed that elder
abuse was not right. He helped me get the records that
would expose the truth about what happened to Rose
without any financial gain.

I sent the Department of Health investigation report
and the "skilled" nursing facility replies to him. This
was more than one year after we lost Rose. The email
back from him in italics said (note the bold language
in particular):

*Please send me everything you have. If you
have reports from the Department of Health*

*or DSHS. or records or anything relating to the care at "skilled" nursing, I need them. **I clearly don't have a complete file from "skilled" nursing. It is missing records that are required to be in your mother's chart.***

Please print the attached letter. Sign the letter and send it to the address listed for "skilled" nursing. Print another copy, sign it and send it to me at the address on the letter.

*This letter is a newly enacted law meant to simplify obtaining your own records or if the resident is deceased, for the relatives of the deceased person to get their records. **You can expect to get correspondence back that questions your right to get records.** Please forward that correspondence to me and I will respond to "skilled" nursing to try and get them to comply with the request or records."*

Our lawyer was right. People at "skilled" nursing resisted the request for the records. After this letter was sent, they actually hired a lawyer to delay releasing the records. They dragged their feet and said that both my brother and I had to request the records. Our lawyer sent a form for us both to sign that went to the lawyer for "skilled" nursing. Now they had to produce. The Department of Health investigation had not bothered to get the hospital records. I did request those after another helpful lawyer advised me to do so. The people at the hospital did not stall and delay as "skilled" nursing had.

More than a year after Rose left this world, I was still trying to get the medical records for her. The delay gave the guilty parties their escape route. It gave them time to enhance the Cover Up. Unfortunately for Rose, I was not able to help her in time. We all trusted the "skilled" nursing RNs, staff, and the doctors. We had no idea how they planned to let her die.

Cover Up in Full Force

The RN who hurt Rose that morning on August 16 when Rose was desperately seeking help was fired on August 23. That didn't bring Rose back. She was fired after I broke the news at "skilled" nursing on August 21 that we found out at the hospital that Rose had indeed suffered a stroke and not a UTI. The "skilled" nursing people claimed they fired that RN for abusing another resident, not Rose.

The Cover Up remained in full motion.

This is the lesson to learn from my mother: *You must get access to medical records immediately when there is any kind of medical situation.* That means all records from any hospital, nursing home, and/or health care facility. If you don't, it may be too late to save or help the one you love. *The law gives you these rights.* You have the right to review and receive copies too.

Do not be dissuaded by those who don't want you to have access. Take immediate access every day when you or someone you love is under the care of a medical provider. Don't trust the hospital personnel or "skilled" nursing home officials. Review the records. They may not like it; but it's the law.

I didn't realize we could do that, and I didn't think we needed to. We trusted them all.

What follows is the law about your health information rights that can help you.

7

Your Health Information Rights

The Health Insurance Portability and Accountability Act of 1996 (HIPAA) Privacy Rule provides you with health information privacy rights. Your health information rights include:

- Right to access your health information
- Right to an accounting of disclosures of your health information
- Right to correct or amend your health information
- Right to notice of privacy practices
- Right to file a complaint

The HIPAA Privacy Rule gives you the right to inspect, review, and receive a copy of your health and billing records that are held by health plans and health care providers covered under HIPAA.[21]

---

21   Not all facilities where you live or stay as you grow older may be considered health care providers. A "skilled" nursing facility is a nursing home that satisfies the requirements for Medicare and Medicaid payments. Nursing care must be available 24 hours a day. A doctor is supposed to supervise the

HIPAA provides each patient with the right to inspect his or her record and to have a copy of the record. These are two different things. You cannot be charged a fee if you want to inspect your records. This means that you can always see your record, even if you don't want to pay.

There are many reasons you might want to review your health record at your health care provider or insurer. For instance:

- You plan to move to another city and want to bring your records to a new doctor so that the doctor has your current information on your first visit. You may not know who the new doctor is in advance so you cannot arrange a doctor-to-doctor transfer.

- You want a second opinion from another doctor and want to avoid having duplicate tests. If you have the records, you don't have to let your first doctor know about the second opinion.

- You want to make sure that your new consulting doctor knows about earlier treatments and previous tests.

- You want to keep a permanent copy of all your health records in one place and in your possession.

---

medical care. This is a big flaw in many nursing homes, so do not be fooled. There may be a medical director "named," but likely he or she will be absent most of the time. Assisted living facilities are for those persons who can take care of themselves to a certain extent. There typically is not medical assistance 24 hours a day. They may assist with some of the activities of daily life (ADLS).

- You are curious.
- You want to make sure that your children have your records because you think that something in your record (e.g., genetic information or family history that they may not know) may eventually be relevant to their treatment.
- You have given your medical power of attorney to your grandson, and you want him to have all of your records (not just those for your current treatment) so that he can make informed decisions or so he can obtain assistance in making choices. By the way, the records that you give to your grandson are not covered by HIPAA in his hands (except, perhaps, if he is a physician or other health care provider).
- You want to talk to a lawyer about medical malpractice and don't want your health care provider to know about it.
- You think that there might be incorrect or irrelevant information in your record.
- You think that you are a victim of medical identity theft.
- You think that your insurance company improperly denied your claim, and you want to see the record about you that the company maintains.
- You think that your doctor or insurance company is lying to you.
- Any other reason or no reason. It is your right to see or have a copy of your record. You don't

need to have a reason or tell anyone what your reason is.

In a few special cases, you may not be able to get all of your information. For example, your doctor may decide that something in your file could physically endanger you or someone else and may not have to give this information to you.

In most cases, your copies must be given to you within 30 days. However, if your health information is not maintained or accessible on-site, your health care provider or health plan can take up to 60 days to respond to your request. If, for some reason, they cannot take action by these deadlines, your provider or plan may extend the deadline by another 30 days if they give you a reason for the delay in writing and tell you when to expect your copies.

The provider cannot charge a fee for searching for or retrieving your information, but you may have to pay for the cost of copying and mailing. Many health care providers—particularly those still using paper-based systems—may not have all of your records available immediately, so it might take them a while to fulfill your request.

If your health care provider keeps your records electronically, you have a right to receive them in either electronic or paper form.

Depending on your doctor's or hospital's policies, you may have to make requests for health information in writing.

Who has to follow the parts of the HIPAA privacy rule that give me rights with respect to my health information?

- Most doctors, nurses, pharmacies, hospitals, clinics, nursing homes, and many other health care providers
- Health insurance companies, Health Maintenance Organization (HMOs), and most employer group health plans
- Certain government programs that pay for health care, such as Medicare and Medicaid

Do I have the right to file a complaint?

Yes. If you believe your information was used or shared in a way that is not allowed under the HIPAA Privacy Rule, or if you were not able to exercise your health information rights, you can file a complaint with your provider or health insurer. The privacy Notice you receive from them will tell you how to file a complaint. You can also file a complaint with the U.S. Department of Health and Human Services (HHS) Office for Civil Rights or your State's Attorneys General office.

Are state governments involved in protecting privacy rights?

Yes. The HIPAA Privacy Rule sets a federal "floor" of privacy protections—a minimum level of privacy that health care providers and health plans must meet. Many states have health information privacy laws that have additional protections that are above this floor. In addition, even though HIPAA is a federal law, State Attorneys General have been given the authority to enforce HIPAA.

How do you make your request?
For each provider from whom you wish to receive records, prepare to make your request by writing down what information you want and how you would like to receive it. Think about the following questions:

- Are you looking for all the information your provider has about you, or for specific information about, for example, a particular condition or office visit?
- What type of information are you looking for? You can ask for any or all types of information in your medical records, including:
  o summary of the office visit,
  o diagnoses,
  o doctors' notes,
  o laboratory results,
  o medication information,
  o images (X-rays, MRIs, etc.); and
  o account and billing information.
- Do you want your records on paper or electronically (if available)? If you want them electronically, how do you want to receive them (via the web, on a flash drive, on a CD, etc.)? Note that

your provider may not be able to support your preferred format.

Adopted in 2013 is the requirement that you can tell a covered entity to transmit your record directly to someone you designate. Your request must be in writing, signed, and clearly identify the designated person and where to send the copy of protected health information. We think this rule was needed because some hospitals made it hard for a patient's lawyer to obtain the patient's record.

How much will it cost?
A covered entity can charge a reasonable, cost-based fee for providing a copy. The fee may include only the cost of labor for copying, the cost of supplies for creating the paper copy or electronic media, and the cost of postage. Any other copying charges—including but not limited to administrative fees, overhead, retrieval costs for locating data—are improper. Charges for inspecting a record are improper, even if the covered entity says that it had to make a copy for you to inspect. Charges for a summary or for an explanation are permissible if you ask for a summary or explanation.

Don't let anyone charge you more than is allowed by the HIPAA rule. If you don't think that the fees are proper, complain about it. You have a right to complain to the Secretary of HHS (via the Office of Civil Rights). State law may provide for lower fees than HIPAA.

8

Importance of an Autopsy

One of the most important records you will need is an autopsy report—something you may not think of when you lose someone you love. But if there has been a wrongful death, you need this report.

One of the lawyers who helped me was a former nurse. She did advise me to get all the hospital records in addition to the records from the "skilled" nursing facility. As an experienced lawyer, she knew how the game was played in medical neglect cases. Her first question to me was whether I had an autopsy done on Rose, which I didn't. I was so shocked that morning when I received the call to say she was gone, I didn't think of getting an autopsy. The mortuary didn't ask if we wanted one. No one mentioned it. Without it, there was no exact way to prove the cause of death.

The medical director for the nursing home signed her death certificate, even though he never came to see her. He could put down whatever he wanted for the cause of death.

He put down "aspiration"—the easiest thing for

them to Cover Up. He didn't put down "incorrect diagnosis" and "wrong medical treatment." Nor did he list
the actual physical and emotional harm they inflicted
on her, which led to her death.

How could a doctor who never saw a patient be
sure of Rose's cause of death? What he stated on her
death certificate was designed to protect all of the
guilty parties.

This was the Cover Up. It's exactly what the insurance defense lawyer focused on and paid their experts
to lie about.

That's why the former nurse turned elder law lawyer
asked if an autopsy had been performed. Without it,
she could not take the case. She knew that the "skilled"
nursing doctors and their experts would all lie. She was
right; they did.

In fact, the further along we moved the case for
Rose, the more the expert lied. Paid to lie by the
insurance company for "skilled" nursing, that's what
happened. These experts all make a really nice fee.
The risk to lose was too great for the "skilled" nursing
facility and its insurance company. For the world to
find out what they had done to Rose was a huge risk,
so it was dollars well spent to pay their expert to lie.
This expert was even a "respectable" member of the
faculty of medical school. (Insurance defense lawyers
figure that a jury will believe an expert from a medical
school faculty.)

Don't be naïve and think cases like this don't

happen. We were so numb with disbelief the morning Rose passed away, we didn't think about an autopsy. Rose wanted to live and kept fighting to stay alive. Unfortunately, the odds they'd stacked against her were too great.

PART THREE

Your Story Will Help Many

We miss you and love you, Rose.
You are not forgotten.

We think about you always,
We talk about you still,
You have never been forgotten,
And you never will.
(unknown author)

Here's the shawl I put around your shoulders to keep you well on August 15, 2012—our last good day together. I wish it could have protected you.

Rose, your memory will live on through all the people who will be helped by your story.

Acknowledgments

First, to Mom who never left me and who gave me the strength to write this story. From the moment they said "she's gone," I knew she was not gone in spirit. Never give up on someone you love.

Second, to my two dear and wise retired doctor friends, Elmer and Stephen, who early on gave me the validation to seek the answer to Mom's death. They knew I was not crazy about what happened. Their experience and message to me confirmed that she had indeed suffered and others were at fault. It gave me the determination to carry on with my fight for justice. They didn't doubt me when others did.

Finally, to my editor Barbara McNichol, who helped me bring this story to you. An absolutely amazing editor who really understood my story and helped me present it better. She made it complete and gave me confidence this was an important message. A pleasure to work with. I was lucky to find her.

Appendix A

Email From a Retired Doctor and Friend

Monday, August 12, 2013, at 2:18 p.m.

Subject: Comments

What you have written up does not surprise me, having seen it all. Sad to say, what is shown in these records is not that far from the standard of care existing in community level nursing homes. I'll opt for private nurses in my home for me personally! Or at least pay for full time private nurses if ever seriously ill, even while in a nursing home.

Medicare forces hospitals to eject patients to a nursing home much sooner now under current rules than in the past when I practiced hospital medicine (called by Medicare DRGs, diagnosis related guidelines). I doubt that much will be accomplished by complaint to an administrative body. What can they do? Shut them all down?

Perhaps you should be focusing more strongly on another more important legal point: actionable harm to the patient. The record seems to show that that your mother was apparently force-fed by mouth (pudding) at a time when she could not swallow because a stroke had recently paralyzed her swallowing muscles. If so, some of the food would have gone into the lungs instead of the stomach. The cough and gag reflex would have been lost or reduced after a stroke. This would have resulted in aspiration into the lungs during needed inhalation of air, and also blunted the reflex to cough it back out, which then could lead to pneumonia. That could not have occurred if she had been fed only by IV or stomach tube, without having the easily aspirated foods (or even liquids) forced into her mouth when she could not swallow.

Appendix B

Denying Payment for Unnecessary Emergency Room Visits

Douglas Perednia, MD | Policy | March 5, 2012

Just when American healthcare system seems so dysfunctional that it seems impossible to imagine how it could be screwed up further, a decision is made that restores one's faith in the creativity of Man. But before you run out of guesses as to which particular decision we're talking about today, we'll just blurt it out. We are referring to a recent decision by *Washington State Medicaid to deny payment for emergency room evaluations* incurred by its beneficiaries that this public insurance entity decides were, in retrospect, "unnecessary."

No "three strikes you're out", no quibbling over the diagnosis list, no excuses – Medicaid has washed its hands of these people. We'd previous written about this story, when the folks at Washington Medicaid were just getting warmed up at the end of 2011. Little did we know we'd be revisiting the issue so soon. Have the people running the Medicaid program in Washington State gone nuts?

Like nearly all public healthcare insurers, Medicaid in the great state of Washington is rapidly going broke. The state is faced with a $1.4 billion budget gap in the FY 2011-2013 biennial state budget, and has begun cutting all sorts of benefits to its Medicaid population. But these pale in comparison with the innovation the state has devised in terms of saving on its annual Medicaid emergency room bill. It's a program which, as nearly as we can tell, hasn't yet been tried elsewhere. Call it "Heads We Win, Tails You Lose."

Here's the story from the *Seattle Times*:

Intent on cutting state budget health-care costs, Medicaid officials say the program will no longer pay for any medically unnecessary emergency-room visits, *even when patients or parents have reason to believe they're having an emergency.*

The rules—arguably more drastic than an earlier proposal to limit Medicaid patients to three visits per year for nonemergency conditions—would block payment for ER visits for about 500 different conditions.

They would apply to all adults and children on Medicaid, with no exceptions, such as someone being brought in by ambulance or from a nursing home, or when patients have neurological symptoms or unstable vital signs.

Of course the need for some sort of action to be taken is pretty straightforward: a certain number of Washington Medicaid patients are clearly abusing the system and costing taxpayers millions in the process. Under the new rules, ER services not paid by Medicaid wouldn't be billed to the patient, leaving the doctor or hospital on the hook.

For those of you who may not be familiar with the ins and outs of emergency rooms, federal law mandates that each and every person walking into one be seen and evaluated regardless of their ability to pay. This is a result of the Emergency Medical Treatment and Active Labor Act (EMTALA), which was passed by Congress in 1986.

It may not have occurred to Dr. Thompson and the other folks in charge of this "innovation," but it seems self-evident that when a person repeatedly goes to an emergency room for problems that are not medically urgent, we are really talking about a social problem rather than a medical one. Heck, other states have recognized this reality. Oregon has launched a very useful and cost-effective program (that essentially assigns a social worker to each high-cost Medicaid recipient. What the new Washington Medicaid program does is simply convert a social problem to an economic one, and then dump it on doctors and hospitals in the private sector. If this is the best government thinkers can do, we are all in some serious trouble. Heads should roll as a result of pulling this sort of stunt. Where's the Queen of Hearts when you really need her?

We may have already crossed that line.

Doug Perednia, M.D. is a medical internist and dermatologist who has been a clinician, healthcare researcher, entrepreneur and employer. Originally trained in Economics at Swarthmore College, he received his medical degree from Washington University in St. Louis, Missouri. This was followed by residencies in internal medicine and dermatology.

Appendix C

Care Suffers as More Nursing Homes Feed Money into Corporate Webs

By Jordan Rau December 31, 2017 KHN Original

MEMPHIS, Tenn. – When one of Martha Jane Pierce's sons peeled back the white sock that had been covering his 82-year-old mother's right foot for a month, he discovered rotting flesh.

"It looked like a piece of black charcoal" and smelled "like death," her daughter Cindy Hatfield later testified. After Pierce, a patient at a Memphis nursing home, was transferred to a hospital, a surgeon had to amputate much of her leg.

One explanation for Pierce's lackluster care, according to financial records and testimony in a lawsuit brought by the Pierce family, is that her nursing home, Allenbrooke Nursing and Rehabilitation Center, appeared to be severely underfunded at the time, with a $2 million deficit on its books in 2009 and a scarcity of nurses and aides. "Sometimes we'd be short of diapers, sheets, linens," one nurse testified.

That same year, $2.8 million of the facility's $12 million in operating expenses went to a constellation of corporations controlled by two Long Island accountants who, court records show, owned Allenbrooke and 32 other nursing homes. The homes paid the men's other companies to provide physical therapy, management, drugs and other services, from which the owners reaped profits, according to court records.

In what has become an increasingly common business arrangement, owners of nursing homes outsource a wide variety of goods and services to companies in which they have a financial interest or that they control. Nearly three-quarters of nursing homes in the United States—more than 11,000—have such business dealings, known as related party transactions, according to an analysis of nursing home financial records by Kaiser Health News. Some homes even contract out basic functions like management or rent their own building from a sister corporation, saying it is simply an efficient way of running their businesses and can help minimize taxes.

But these arrangements offer another advantage: Owners can establish highly favorable contracts in which their nursing homes pay more than they might in a competitive market. Owners then siphon off higher profits, which are not recorded on the nursing home's accounts.

The two Long Island men, Donald Denz and Norbert Bennett, and their families' trusts collected distributions totaling $40 million from their chain's $145 million in revenue over eight years—a 28 percent margin, according to the judge's findings of fact. In 2014 alone, Denz earned $13 million and Bennett made $12 million, principally from their nursing home companies, according to personal income tax filings presented in court.

Typical nursing home profits are "in the 3 to 4 percent range," said Bill Ulrich, a nursing home financial consultant.

In 2015, nursing homes paid related companies $11 billion, a tenth of their spending, according to financial disclosures the homes submitted to Medicare.

In California, the state auditor is examining related party transactions at another nursing home chain, Brius Healthcare Services. Rental prices to the chain's real estate entities were a third higher than rates paid by other for-profit nursing homes in the same counties, according to an analysis by the National Union of Healthcare Workers.

Such corporate webs bring owners a legal benefit, too: When a nursing home is sued, injured residents and their families have a much harder time collecting money from the related companies—the ones with the full coffers.

After the Pierce family won an initial verdict against the nursing home, Denz and Bennett appealed, and their lawyer, Craig Conley, said they would not discuss details of the case or their business while the appeal was pending.

"For more than a decade, Allenbrooke's caregivers have promoted the health, safety and welfare of their residents," Conley wrote in an email.

Dr. Michael Wasserman, the head of the management company for the Brius nursing homes, called corporate structures a "nonissue" and said, "What matters at the end of the day is what the care being delivered is about."

Networks of jointly owned limited liability corporations are fully legal and used widely by other businesses, such as restaurants and retailers. Nonprofit nursing homes sometimes use them as well. Owners can have more control over operations—and better allocate resources—if they own all the companies. In many cases, industry consultants say, a commonly owned company will charge a nursing home lower fees than an independent contractor might, leaving the chain with more resources.

"You don't want to pay for someone else to make money off of you," Ulrich said. "You want to retain that within your organization."

But a Kaiser Health News analysis of federal inspection and quality records reveals that nursing homes that outsource to related organizations tend to have significant shortcomings: They have fewer nurses and aides per patient, they have higher rates of patient injuries and unsafe practices, and they are the subject of complaints almost twice as often as independent homes.

"Almost every single one of these chains is doing the same thing," said Charlene Harrington, a professor emeritus of the School of Nursing at the University of California-San Francisco. "They're just pulling money away from staffing."

Early Signs of Trouble

Martha Jane Pierce moved to Allenbrooke in 2008 in the early stages of dementia. According to testimony in the family's lawsuit, her children often discovered her unwashed when they visited, with an uneaten, cold meal sitting beside her bed. Hatfield said in court that she had frequently found her mother's bed soaked in urine. The front desk was sometimes vacant, her brother Glenn Pierce testified.

"If you went in on the weekend, you'd be lucky to find one nurse there," he said in an interview.

After a stroke, Pierce became partly paralyzed and nonverbal, but the nursing home did not increase the attention she received, said Carey Acerra, one of Pierce's lawyers. When Pierce's children visited, they rarely saw aides reposition her in bed every two hours, the standard practice to prevent bedsores.

"Not having enough staffing, we can't—we weren't actually able to go and do that," one nurse, Cheryl Gatlin-Andrews, testified in a deposition.

KHN's analysis of federal inspection, staffing and financial records nationwide found shortcomings at other homes with similar corporate structures:

Homes that did business with sister companies employed, on average, 8 percent fewer nurses and aides. As a group, these homes were 9 percent more likely to have hurt residents or put them in immediate jeopardy of harm, and amassed 53 validated complaints for every 1,000 beds, compared with the 32 per 1,000 that inspectors found credible at independent homes. Homes with related companies were fined 22 percent more often for serious health violations than were independent homes, and penalties averaged $24,441—7 percent higher.

For-profit nursing homes employ these related corporations more frequently than nonprofits do, and have fared worse than independent for-profit homes in fines, complaints and staffing, the analysis found. Their fines averaged $25,345, which was 10 percent higher than fines for independent for-profits, and the homes received 24 percent more substantiated complaints from residents. Overall staffing was 4 percent lower than at independent for-profits.

Ernest Tosh, a plaintiffs' lawyer in Texas who helps other lawyers untangle nursing company finances, said owners often exerted control by setting tight budgets that restricted the number of nurses the homes could employ. Meanwhile, "money is siphoned out to these related parties," he said. "The cash flow gets really obscured through the related party transactions."

The American Health Care Association, which represents nursing homes, disputed any link between related businesses and poor care. "Our members strive to provide quality care at an affordable cost to every resident," the group said in a statement. "There will always be examples of exceptions, but those few do not represent the majority of our profession."

'Piercing the Corporate Veil'

The model of placing nursing homes and related businesses in separate limited liability corporations and partnerships has gained popularity as the industry has consolidated through purchases by publicly traded companies, private investors and private equity firms. A 2003 article in the Journal of Health Law encouraged owners to separate their nursing home business into detached entities to protect themselves if the government tried to recoup overpayments or if juries levied large negligence judgments.

"Holding the real estate in a separate real-property entity that leases the nursing home to the operating entity protects the assets by making the real estate unavailable for collection by judgment creditors of the operating entity," the authors wrote. Such restructuring, they added, was probably not worth it just for "administrative simplicity."

In 2009, Harvard Medical School researchers found the practice had flourished among nursing homes in Texas, which they studied because of the availability of state data. Owners had also inserted additional corporations between them and their nursing homes, with many separated by three layers.

To bring related companies into a lawsuit, attorneys must persuade judges that all the companies were essentially acting as one entity and that the nursing home could not make its own decisions. Often that requires getting access to internal company documents and emails. Even harder is holding owners personally responsible for the actions of a corporation—known as "piercing the corporate veil."

At a 2012 Nashville conference for executives in the long-term health care industry, a presentation slide from nursing home attorneys titled "Pros of Complex Corporate Structure" stated: "Many plaintiffs' attorneys will never conduct corporate structure discovery because it's too expensive and time consuming." The presentation noted another advantage: "Financial statement in punitive damages phase shows less income and assets."

A lawyer in Alabama, Barry Walker, is still fighting an 11-year-old case against another nursing home then owned by Denz and Bennett, according to court records. Walker traced the ownership of Fairfield Nursing and Rehabilitation Center back to the men, but he said the judge had allowed him to introduce the ownership information only after the Alabama Supreme Court ordered him. That trial ended with a hung jury, and Walker said a subsequent judge had not let him present all the information to two other juries, and he dropped the men from the lawsuit. The home closed a few years ago but the case is still ongoing despite two mistrials.

"The former trial judge and the current trial judge quite frankly don't seem to understand piercing the corporate veil," he said. "My firm invested more in the case than we can ever hope to recover. Sometimes it's a matter of principle."

The complexity of the ownership in Pierce's case was a major reason it took six years to get to a trial, said Ken Connor, one of the lawyers for her family. "It requires a lot of digging to unearth what's really going on," he said. "Most lawyers can't afford to do that."

The research paid off in a rare result: In 2016, the jury issued a $30 million verdict for negligence, of which Denz and Bennett were personally liable for $20 million. The men's own tax returns bolstered the case against them. They claimed during trial they delegated daily responsibilities for residents to the home's administrators, but they reported on their tax returns that they "actively" participated in the management. The jury did not find the nursing home responsible for Pierce's death later in 2009.

The fight is not over. Denz and Bennett are appealing the verdict, the damages, their inclusion and the trial judge's decisions. They argue that Tennessee courts should not have jurisdiction over them since they spent little time in the state and neither was involved in the daily operations of the home or in setting staffing levels. Their lawyers said jurors should never have heard from nurses who hadn't cared directly for Pierce.

"No way did I oversee resident care issues," Bennett testified in a deposition.

Deficient in the End

Whoever was responsible for Pierce's care, her family had no doubt it was inadequate. Her son Bill Pierce was so horrified when he finally saw the wound on his mother's foot, he immediately insisted that she go to the hospital.

"The surgeon said he had never seen anything like it," Hatfield said in an interview. "He amputated 60 percent of the leg, above the knee."

After her amputation, Pierce returned to the nursing home because her family did not want to separate her from her husband, who was also there.

At the trial, the nursing home's lawyers argued that Pierce's leg had deteriorated not because of the infection but because her blood vessels had become damaged from a decline in circulation. The jury was unpersuaded after nurses and aides testified about how Allenbrooke would add staffing for state inspections while the rest of the time their pleas for more support went unheeded.

Workers also testified that supervisors had told them to fill in blanks in medical records regardless of accuracy. One example: Allenbrooke's records indicated that Pierce had eaten a full meal the day after she died.

Increasingly, owners of nursing homes outsource services to companies in which they also have financial interest or control. That allows the nursing homes to claim to be in the red while owners reap hidden profits.

Data journalist Elizabeth Lucas contributed to this report. khn.org.

Kaiser Health News is a nonprofit news service covering health issues. It is an editorially independent program of the Kaiser Family Foundation that is not affiliated with Kaiser Permanente.

Appendix D

Important for Your Estate Plan

An Executor/Executrix (male/female) is the individual appointed by a will to handle the personal and financial matters of a person after their death. An Executor is the legal personal representative of the deceased person's estate. A loved one's wrongful death can be the basis for a lawsuit filed on behalf of the estate by the Executor for the estate.

Everyone should have a will to name the individual you trust the most to handle your matters after your death. If you die without a will, the probate court will appoint your closest living relative as the Executor.

My brother Kelly and I were Rose's only living relatives. Kelly consented to me being named Executrix. It is best to have your will name your Executor to avoid any potential disputes among relatives after your death. Unfortunately, family disputes after death is common in many families.

Executor: An Executor is the person who takes care of your affairs after you die. Remember, a general or durable power of attorney names a person to handle matters for you only while you are alive.

Probate: **Probate** is the judicial process wherein a deceased individual's assets are administered and distributed to the beneficiaries named in the will or by the law of intestate succession (the court determines who are legally the closest family members entitled to inherit) if there is no will.

Revocable Living Trust: For those fortunate to have substantial assets, often a revocable living trust (it can be amended or revoked during lifetime) is done with a will. The living trust holds title to an individual's assets during their lifetime, and then after an individual's death, the trust becomes irrevocable and administers and distributes the assets of the deceased person without the expense or delay of probate. The person handling the trust is the Trustee. The Executor and Trustee may be the same person.

Forms for will and revocable living trusts are available online. However, it is easy to make mistakes if you do your own legal documents. It is recommended you hire a professional to help you.

Appendix E

My Life Plan Questionnaire & Checklist

Introduction:

Appendix E is added to the Second Edition of the book as a helpful bonus to readers. As the author, I experienced in the first six months of the book's publication and release, a tremendous positive response from readers, clients and professionals. People stood in line after seminars to have me sign the book for them and copies for their children. Professionals in estate planning and elder law responded finding the book a motivating force to get clients to move beyond their estate plan and begin to plan for their aging years.

After people read the book, they ask me what they should do to get better prepared for growing older. One reader aptly said: "the book made me sad, then mad, then apprehensive." I decided that I didn't want readers to be left feeling apprehensive. Instead, I wanted to offer them a solution.

When I speak to groups, I ask the audience: "What is your life plan?" It gets them thinking, but they don't know what to do. So, nothing happens. We put off our important things for another day. We believe we have another good day to do those important things. That isn't always the case. Emergencies, sudden illness or accidents can happen at any time. After 40 years of doing estate planning, I know how a crisis can arise when you least expect it and are the least prepared.

I realized that readers need a checklist to work on now; a questionnaire for planning their own life and care after they read this book. There already are advance care planning checklists, but those lists focus on health care decisions alone, and more directed toward end of life planning. Planning does not mean you have to be old. It applies for all adults in all stages of their life. This questionnaire and checklist does more than plan your health care. It is your life plan. The journal about your life.

Below are the questions and a checklist to complete. This is the period from today to the end of your life. These are your last chapters, however many there may be. Plan them now yourself. Don't let someone else plan them for you. Remember, this is your life plan.

Dear Reader: This questionnaire and checklist is to be completed and *updated regularly.*

If you don't update it, you hurt yourself. This is your chance to put your thoughts and wishes on paper to have them understood and followed by others. *It is the journal for your life.*

Instructions to Follow: As you work on the questions and checklist, please print clearly. When you complete the checklist, make copies and distribute a copy to others who should have all or part of your checklist. You can begin your discussion with these trusted people through these questions and checklist. Let them read over your choices and understand better who you are. My Life Plan is an easy step to begin those difficult discussions with family or friends about legal documents, medical care, where you want to live as you age, and your end of life choices.

Communication skills are often not good within families. People may drop hints instead of asking or stating a request directly. No one can accurately reader another person's mind. So many things go unsaid or unanswered. We are afraid we will be criticized, judged or ignored. As an adult, we don't want to lose our independence or control. It happens as we age unfortunately. People often show more interest and empathy with strangers and animals instead of their own family. As the Mills Brother's popular song says: "You always hurt the one you <u>love</u>, the one you should not hurt at all. You always take the sweetest rose, and crush it till the petals fall; You always break the kindest heart, with a hasty word you can't recall".

With this questionnaire and checklist, it can be a new beginning. This checklist is a good opener for families to talk with each other about the important things in life while they can. Even a little dialogue is better than none.

If you have no family to rely on, and must find friends or senior advisors to help you, start now and begin this process with them.

After you finish the checklist and begin your discussions, schedule the next review for any updates and discussions. A suggested review is at least every six months or sooner if there is a change in health or personal circumstances. Plan this review with your professional advisor too.

Once a page becomes full in this book, start with a new blank piece of paper for that page and keep it with the book. Initial and date beside a question on the checklist each time you modify it or on a new page. See below under legal documents for suggestions on how to have this checklist, My Life Plan, honored and a part of your advance directives or estate plan. You may also download and print a new My Life Plan Questionnaire and Checklist at:

www.seniorcarepublising.com

To print, type in the code: 2019Rose

Comments are made after some of the questions to provide you valuable information and insights from the author to consider.

My Life Plan Questionnaire & Checklist

1. My Complete Legal Name and any other name(s) that I go by or use to sign documents and my current address:

2. Date My Life Plan Questionnaire & Checklist is completed the first time and each update:

Legal Documents

3. **My Estate Plan** is a (check which apply and date when done and when last updated):

Will _____

Date

Main purpose: Identifies all family members who might inherit from you by choice or by operation of the law; distributes assets not titled in a trust; names the executor for your estate; names the guardian for minors; does not avoid probate and may provide estate tax savings if a drafted for those rules. A will is effective upon your death.

Not to be confused with a living will. The living will is a legal document valid during your lifetime for your health care decisions and wishes.

Living Trust _____

Date

Main purpose: Assets titled in the name of the trust avoid probate; provides privacy from the public re your assets and family at death; may serve to *avoid having a guardian appointed for you* as you age or become incapacitated. This avoidance of a guardianship is a very important planning opportunity. You name someone you trust to act as the trustee with you or for you in the event of your incapacity so a guardian is not appointed. The trust should provide for this in lieu of a guardian in the written document.

The trust is revocable and can be amended or canceled during your life. All the assets belong to you and are taxable to you during your life. There can be estate tax savings if drafted for those rules. You are the trustee and sign so you control the assets. You need to have a trusted advisor, family member or friend who can act as the successor trustee or co-trustee when you cannot act or upon your death.

A living trust needs a will to name the executor for the estate. Both documents have formal execution requirements in every state.

Laws vary from state to state on the fiduciary duties and accountability of trustees and protectors. Protectors are usually someone you trust and are named in a trust to generally see that your wishes are followed. State laws differ on the role of protectors. It is important to review these decisions with your attorney to make sure the trust provides for a method to review and remove/replace a trustee or protector.

Consult with your attorney when you do your will and/or living trust to make sure the documents are prepared and executed correctly. If the living trust makes reference to and incorporates this checklist, the checklist can become a part of your legal documents and not just a personal note. This reference to include and incorporate this checklist can also be made a part of your living will and/or durable power of attorney below and may be the better place to include the checklist.

Irrevocable Trust _____

Date

Main Purpose: To remove assets from your owner-ship for tax purposes and Medicaid planning purposes. Normally a gift is made to the trust to create the trust and to move ownership of the gifted assets away from you. You name other persons or entities to be the bene-ficiaries of the trust and when they can receive any dis-tributions. Trust is permanent and can be amended or terminated only with very narrow provisions drafted into the trust that keep your ownership removed from the trust. Often used for Medicaid planning; estate tax planning to keep life insurance proceeds out of your taxable estate; and by foreigners to keep US assets out of their taxable estate. Medicaid planning trusts may provide you an income stream but not control over the principal. Medicaid planning trusts are very popular and generally require at least a 5 year period (look back) to pass after a gift is made to the trust. You need a trusted advisor, friend or family member to be the trustee. As with the living trust explanation above, be careful with the selection of a trustee and protec-tor. They may have more control with an irrevocable trust, so it is important to have drafting done by your attorney. An experienced attorney or advisor in elder law and Medicaid planning is recommended to help you.

4.   **My Advance Directives** are (check which apply and date when signed and when updated):

Living Will _____

Date

If you have no one to act as your health care agent under a durable power of attorney (below), the living will is the best method to communicate your choices for your health care. This makes it a very important document to keep current. Each state has an online source for a form; but it is recommended you prepare this document with the assistance of both a trained medical and legal professional.

A living will provides more information on your medical choices than a Do Not Resuscitate Form; also known as no CPR, Cardiopulmonary resuscitation. The DNR form is a medical order that communicates a person's desire to forgo cardiopulmonary resuscitation should their heart stop beating and they stop breathing.

In some states, a living will may be referred to as a physician's directive or health care directive. There are many medical choices for you to make on a living will that will keep you alive beyond a sudden death and a do not resuscitate form or no CPR.

Reader Alert! Once you choose a DNR option on a legal or medical document, medical personnel may not look to your other medical choices for something less than a sudden death. The older you are, medical personnel may focus more on the DNR option if you chose that. You must be very clear in your medical choices in all documents. As an example, a feeding tube may not be a choice made by a younger healthy person on a medical or legal form. If you have a medical emergency or become seriously ill, a temporary feeding tube may save your life. Make sure you fully understand the health care choices that you make and review them regularly.

Durable power of attorney for health care _____

Remember: If a power of attorney is durable, it remains valid and in effect even if you become incapacitated and unable to make decisions for yourself. If a power of attorney document does not explicitly say that the power is durable, it ends if you become incapacitated. A power of attorney of any kind is only valid while you are alive. The agent named has no power to act after your death. A Durable Power of Attorney can be for health and financial decisions. Warning! Many states are adopting laws which allow a court appointed guardian to cancel a power of attorney agent. Make sure your Durable Power is created to eliminate a guardianship if you do not want a guardian appointed.

Main Purpose: A person is named under the durable power of attorney as your agent, who can make medical decisions for you <u>if</u> you are too ill or incapacitated to make your own decisions. This person becomes your health care agent. Sometimes this person is called your health care proxy. You can designate this person or persons to start making decisions for you whenever you want. If you name more than one person, such as several children or friends, decide if they must agree and act together or can act alone. State laws on powers of attorney are changing and may require joint decision making unless otherwise designated. You should seek advice from your attorney and possibly update your existing power of attorney for health care.

Date and name of health care agent (person or persons named in power of attorney) with contact details:

I have made detailed health care choices in the durable power for health care rather than leaving those choices to my health care agent. Please Print Yes or No:

I have discussed my durable power for health care and my choices with my health care agent. Please Print Yes or No:

I have completed a HIPPA Right of Access form to have my health care agent and/or others have access to my medical records. This is very important to get in place now and to keep current for those individuals who shall have access to and receive your medical records. See sample HIPPA letter at the end of the Appendices. Please Print Yes or No:

I have a combined durable power for both health care and finances. Please Print Yes or No:

The same person or persons are named to act as my agent for health care and finances. Please Print Yes or No:

I have the originals of my advance directives kept safely where they can be found easily and quickly, and my agents named above all have copies. I realize that these documents may not be readily available in a medical emergency unless I carry an advance directive card with me and keep it up to date. If I don't have an advance directive card, I will ask my attorney to prepare one for me. My originals are located:

Durable powers of attorney are a serious and important legal document. It is recommended that you do not try to do one on your own. There are free forms on line, but you can make many serious mistakes.

Many states have recently adopted some form of the Uniform Power of Attorney Act to combat against breaches of fiduciary duties committed by agents named in powers of attorney for health care and/or finances. These breaches extend to trusted friends, family, advisors and religious leaders acting under a power of attorney.

As with the trustee and/or protector above in a trust, it is important to review a power of attorney with your attorney to make sure the document provides for a method to review and remove/replace an agent for health care and/or finances. Make sure you are not creating problems that you will regret by the people you choose to act for you and the powers you give them.

It's all about trust. There are many horror stories about trusted family, friends, parishioners, and advisors who betray a person once they have a power of attorney. Make sure you create yours carefully and review it often for necessary modifications. *The richer, older or sicker you are, the more you are at risk.*

Many of the tragedies you read or hear about with elder abuse happen through critical documents not being completed correctly, the wrong agents appointed or documents not kept current. See the website for senior care publishing to read more details about this: www.seniorcarepublishing.com.

Medical Orders

A POLST may be the most important life or death document for you. Many people do not know what a POLST is. It is a medical order not a legal document. Your recourse to errors made with a POLST may be limited. That is why you must be extra vigilant and diligent with a POLST. Do not take this form for granted.

POLST is known by different names in different states, including MOLST (Medical Orders for Life Sustaining Treatment), MOST (Medical Orders for Scope of Treatment), POST (Physician Orders for Scope of Treatment), LaPOST (Louisiana Physician Order for

Scope of Treatment), COLST (Clinician Orders for Life Sustaining Treatment), IPOST (Iowa Physicians Orders for Scope of Treatment), SMOST (Summary of Physician Orders for Scope of Treatment), TPOPP (Transportable Physician Order for Patient Preference), and WyoPOLST (Wyoming Provider Orders for Life Sustaining Treatment).

The questions on the checklist will use the term POLST to include all of the similar forms from other states.

5. I know what a POLST (Physicians Order for Life Sustaining treatment) is.   Print Yes or No:

6. I now have a POLST, or similar form, signed on this date and from this state. Print Yes or No, and if Yes, print the name of the state:

7. My POLST form choices were explained to me very well by the authorized medical personnel

signing the form with me. Print Yes or No and the name of the authorized medical personnel:

8. The last time I reviewed and updated my POLST was:

9. My POLST is kept at this exact location: (ie, if in your house, where in your house?)

10. A person whom I care about has a POLST form: Print Yes or No, and if Yes, Print the Name of this person, the date the POLST was signed and the name of the authorized medical personnel signing the form:

11. The POLST form choices were explained to the person named in #10 above very well by the authorized medical personnel signing the form. Print if Yes or No:

12. The last time the person in #10 above reviewed their POLST and updated it was:

13. I have a durable power of attorney for health care decisions for the person in #10 above and I have signed and reviewed their POLST on these dates:

14. The POLST for the person in #10 above is kept at this exact location (be specific as with the example in 9 above):

Your doctor or medical care provider should also have a copy of your advance directives and POLST. Make certain they are put in your medical record. Your doctor or medical care provider needs to take the time to speak with you about the important choices you make for your health care and end of life. If your doctor or medical care provider will not take the time to discuss this with you, understand your decisions and agree to honor your choices, you need to find another doctor or medical care provider. Don't wait and don't assume your doctor or medical care provider is on board with you. If in a nursing home, make sure you have your own doctor. The medical director for the nursing home works for them, not for you.

Attention on Medical: As you age, you may discover that people in the medical system lose interest in helping you and making you better. Be alert for this. People tend to have more memories about the past then dreams for the future as they grow older. Comments may be written in your medical records that you are developing dementia. Dementia and Alzheimer's are serious conditions for many older people. But recalling people and times in the past or being a little forgetful does not mean that you have dementia. This dementia label can cause you to be treated unfairly as you age and as you move through the medical system and medical care givers. It is critical that you and your health care agents have access to your medical records at all times.

Conversations about your medical choices and end of life wishes are critical as you age or become ill. This is necessary whether you plan to stay at home and have at home care services, live in an assisted living or senior community, or a nursing home. In today's growing market of senior services, these conversations are particularly important with nursing homes or stay at home health care franchise services where medical care is sometimes fragmented, under trained and under staffed. Be vigilant and diligent at all times.

Personal Matters
Health Concerns, Where I Want To Live and Who Will Help Me

15. I have a serious illness or condition which will shorten my life or may disable me. Print Yes or No, and if Yes, describe that illness or condition:

16. I am of an advanced age and growing frail. Print Yes or No:

17. I have discussed my end of life wishes with someone I trust, who will help me and who will honor my wishes. I have named that person as my agent in my durable power of attorney for health care. Print Yes or No, and if Yes, print the name of the person and their contact details:

18. I have no one I can trust or rely on in #17 to help me and no one named as my agent under a durable power of attorney for health care. Print Yes or No:

19. I have tried to discuss my aging concerns and end of life wishes with my family, but they don't seem interested right now. Print Yes or No:

Younger or healthier family members often have little understanding or appreciation of the aging process and what it is like to grow old. If they are busy working or with their own family, you may get less time and attention. See if the checklist doesn't help you get through to them with your concerns.

20. If I have no one I can trust or rely on to help me in #17 above, I do have a living will and I keep it current. Print Yes or No:

21. I know or I am making plans where I want to live the last years of my life. Print Yes or No, and if Yes, print where that is:

22. I want to stay at home the last years of my life, and can afford to have paid services help me with my day to day living at home (home health care services). Print if Yes or No:

23. I want to live in asst living or a community for seniors so I am not   alone when I grow older and cannot stay at home. Print if Yes or No:

24. I can afford to live in a nice asst living or senior community when I grow older. Print if Yes or No:

25. I will need financial help through Medicaid planning or otherwise to be able to pay for my living and care arrangements as I grow older and cannot stay at home. Print if Yes or No:

Note: If you think you may need to rely on Medicaid for your living arrangements as you age, start looking at places to live early on. Do not rely entirely on referral agencies. Saving money for your family with Medicaid planning is fine; but, you may find yourself in an entirely different life style then you planned.

26. I am worried about my finances to be able to stay at home and pay for help, or live in an assisted living or senior community. Print if Yes or No:

27. I am worried that I may have to live the last years of my life in a nursing home. Print if Yes or No:

28. I am worried that I will not have adequate resources to pay for a nursing home later in my life, or that a nursing home for my spouse will eliminate our resources. Print if Yes or No:

Note: You must be careful when selecting a nursing home for long term care. Many agencies get referral fees for recommending nursing homes. Be warned! Staff is different in the long term care wings of a nursing home from what you may have experienced if you stayed at that nursing home on a Medicare wing for rehab after a hospital stay. This stay up to 30 days paid by Medicare is often a person's first experience with a nursing home. The nurse and aide ratio to residents is usually much lower on the long term care wings. You don't get the same care. When you are on a Medicare wing, you are a visitor and treated better than the long term care "skilled nursing" wing. Once you are on long term care, you are institutionalized.

29. I understand the difference between palliative care and hospice. Print Yes or No. If Yes, indicate if you wish to have palliative care toward the end of your life:

There is a difference between hospice and palliative care. They both provide comfort, but that is all hospice will do. Hospice begins after the treatment of the disease has stopped and it is clear the person will not survive. Usually it is in the last six months of a person's life expectancy that hospice begins care.

Palliative care can begin at the initial diagnosis and during treatment of a serious illness or medical condition. Palliative care focuses on providing relief from the symptoms and stress of a serious illness or medical condition for the person and their family. It improves the quality of life for people of any age and stage of a serious illness even if chronic or life threatening. Palliative care is a specialty in medical training. It is estimated 6 million people in the US could benefit from palliative care now. The Center to Advance Palliative Care estimates the numbers will more than double over the next 25 years as the baby boomers age.

30. I understand that if I want palliative care, I should include that wish in my living will and/or durable power for health care. Print if Yes or No:

31. I have my wishes for either a burial or cremation written down and in either my living will or my durable power for health care. Also included are instructions as to the place of burial or where my ashes are to be spread or kept. Print if Yes or No:

Often the burial or cremation desire is placed by a person in their estate planning documents such as a will. A will may not be found quickly after a death and the burial or cremation may have already occurred.

32. I think it is a good idea to have an autopsy done after my death. Print Yes or No:

33. I have close friends, family or advisors I can rely on to help me in   my later years to make sure I get good care and I am not lonely. Print Yes or No:

34. I have no one to help me in my later years and I will need help. Print Yes or No:

35. I have no plan written down now for anything. No estate plan; no advance directives; no POLST and I need help now to begin to plan! Print Yes or No:

36. I know that dreams don't always come true, but what I hope for in the final years of my life is documented below. I ask that these important things for me be honored and remembered by others:

Statistics show that 90 percent of people say that talking with their loved ones about end of life care is important and only 27 percent have actually done so. (Source: The Conversation Project National Survey, 2013).

Eighty-two percent of people say it's important to put their wishes in writing and 23 percent have actually done it. (Source: Survey of Californians by the California HealthCare Foundation, 2012).

Resources to help you plan: ABA commission on Law and Aging.

SAMPLE FORM

HIPAA Right of Access Form
for Family Member/Friend

I,_____, direct my
health care and medical services providers and payers
to disclose and release my protected health information described below to:

Name:

Relationship:

Contact information:

Health Information to be disclosed upon the request of the person named above -- (Check either A or B):

A. Disclose my complete health record (including but not limited to diagnoses, lab tests, prognosis, treatment, and billing, for all conditions) OR

B. Disclose my health record, as above, BUT do not disclose the following (check as appropriate):
- Mental health records
- Communicable diseases (including HIV and AIDS)
- Alcohol/drug abuse treatment
- Other (please specify):

Form of Disclosure (unless another format is mutually agreed upon between my provider and designee):
- An electronic record or access through an online portal
- Hard copy

This authorization shall be effective until (Check one):
- All past, present, and future periods, OR
- Date or event:_____
- unless I revoke it. (NOTE: You may revoke this

authorization in writing at any time by notifying your health care providers, preferably in writing.)

Name of the Individual Giving this Authorization:

Date of birth:

Signature of the Individual Giving this Authorization:

Date:

Note: HIPAA Authority for Right of Access: 45 C.F.R. § 164.524

About the Author

Karol Charles, JD, LLM, is a tax and estate planning attorney, and for over 40 years has been certified as a tax specialist. She is a former law school, graduate law and business school professor in taxation, and has published and spoken in numerous tax, estate planning, and elder law seminars.

Karol has a BA degree in Economics, a JD degree in Law and a Masters in Law in Taxation.

She can be reached for questions or to arrange a personal consultation by email at:
author@wrongful-death-book.com.

Visit the publisher's website at:
www.seniorcarepublishing.com

Made in the USA
Las Vegas, NV
21 May 2021